The UnGandhian Gandhi

Anthem South Asian Studies
Series Editor: Crispin Bates

The UnGandhian Gandhi :

The Life and Afterlife of the Mahatma

CLAUDE MARKOVITS

Translated from the French
by the author

Anthem Press

This edition published by Anthem Press 2004

Anthem Press is an imprint of
Wimbledon Publishing Company
75-76 Blackfriars Road
London SE1 8HA

or

PO Box 9779, London, SW19 7QA

This edition © Permanent Black 2003 is reprinted by arrangement with the original
publisher and is only for sale outside South Asia

© CLAUDE MARKOVITS 2003

British Library Cataloguing in Publication Data
Data available

Library of Congress in Publication Data
A catalogue record has been applied for

ISBN 1 84331 126 7 (Hbk)
1 84331 127 5 (Pbk)

1 3 5 7 9 10 8 6 4 2

Contents

Preface

This is the English translation of a book I wrote in French, which was published in 2000 by the Presses de Sciences Po. It was part of a still ongoing series of 'non-traditional' biographies of important historical figures. This explains the plan adopted, based on a distinction between perceptions and historical facts. In the series, it had also been decided to keep footnotes to a minimum.

The French text was written with a French audience clearly in mind, and I hoped that it would be of interest to an English-speaking audience. I would like to thank my wife, Piyali, for her careful editing of a former draft.

Paris
March 2004

Introduction

O f all the great figures of the twentieth century, Gandhi has perhaps best stood the test of time. In the aftermath of a century
of unprecedented mass violence, many see in the apostle of
non-violence the prophet of the only possible future for mankind, a
future without hatred, greed and lust for power. Interest in Gandhi's
thought and actions, far from diminishing, is on the increase, and his
message to the world appears uniquely relevant. As more books are
written about him all the time, many see in him a familiar figure and
love the apparent simplicity of his message. He remains, however, in
many ways, an enigma.

One may well ask—Why add a new title to an already overabundant
bibliography? What is there to say about Gandhi that has not already
been said many times over? Writing in praise of him will at best add
one more stone to the already imposing hagiographic edifice built over
several decades by the many priests of the Gandhian cult. Any attempt
at a critical view will be at pains to appear original, as the most feroci-
ous attacks have already been directed towards all aspects of his life and
historical legacy.

In order to avoid being repetitive, one has to find a specific angle
to look at this icon. In this book, two different approaches have been
combined. In the first part, the focus is on existing representations of
Gandhi through a scrutiny of various written texts, and a study of images. Attention is drawn to the emergence of a Gandhian legend, born
during the Mahatma's lifetime and enormously expanded after his
death. In the second part, the focus is on Gandhi's impact upon the
history of the last century, on the manner in which he became a political leader, on his role in India's struggle for freedom, as well as on his
contribution to social reform. More generally, an attempt is made to
situate him within the framework of India's modern history. Lastly,

the theme of non-violence is examined in some detail. So, the aim of this book is not to provide yet one more narrative of Gandhi's life, and in this Introduction only the bare facts of his life and career are outlined.

Born in 1869 in the small princely state of Porbandar in Kathiawar, one of the many Indian states which figure so little in the dominant colonial-oriented historiography of the subcontinent, in a family of merchant caste which served the ruling dynasty, Gandhi was unremarkable till the age of forty. He had an uneventful childhood in Porbandar and in the neighbouring town of Rajkot, even though some episodes of his life, such as his early marriage, were given great prominence in his autobiography and subsequent biographies. His conjugal life, in particular, has come in for a lot of scrutiny and criticism. As a father he has been deemed an outright failure, and it seems difficult to disagree with this view.

His departure for England at the age of nineteen to study law was the first sign of a desire on his part to break away from the established pattern of life as it existed in his milieu. Given his family background—which was not that of the English-educated Indian elite—this seems an early indication of remarkable will power, especially in view of the strict way in which the injunction against crossing the *kala pani* was enforced amongst his Modh *bania* caste fellows. The shy young man found himself suddenly plunged in the whirlwind of the metropolis of empire, and his first response to cultural shock was a particularly frantic attempt at acculturation by aping the ways, dress, and manners of a dandy. Striving to become a perfect gentleman, he discovered vegetarianism and started reading the classic texts of Hinduism in English translations. This helped him to rediscover his own culture, from which he had been somewhat alienated by his lack of Sanskrit. He also acquired a basic knowledge of the law, which would prove highly useful for his future political career. Gandhi's early trajectory resembles that of many Indians of his generation who were torn between two worlds and tried unsuccessfully to acquire a social position in a colonial society where most avenues of advancement were closed to their kin. Having completed his studies, he went back to India in 1891 and tried to pursue a career as a lawyer, but his almost pathological shyness stood in the way of success.

His departure for South Africa in 1893 was to prove the chance of a lifetime, for in the specific colonial context of late-nineteenth-century Natal he was able to find a middle path, equidistant between acculturation and a return to tradition. Hired by a firm of Gujarati Muslim merchants from Porbandar to help them in a court case against another firm of Indian merchants, he was on the verge of going back to India at the expiration of his contract when he was asked by a group of Indian merchants in Durban to help them fight against discriminatory laws. He was to spend another twenty years in South Africa.

Prior to 1906, his story is one of slow learning. The early South African Gandhi was a spokesman for a tiny merchant élite which was clinging to the few privileges which raised it above the mass of indentured labourers that formed the bulk of the South African Indian community. For Gandhi, these were years of intellectual and spiritual maturation; he developed a very idiosyncratic religious faith, which became the source of his strength, and discovered he had hidden talents as an organizer and journalist. His political role remained, in spite of what some of his biographers say, relatively modest prior to 1906. He was involved in the creation of the Indian Natal Congress, but this was not a very active organization. Although he himself displayed real qualities of leadership from the time of his first campaign—waged in 1894 against the suppression of the electoral franchise of the rich Indian merchants in Natal—and showed rare courage—in 1896 he escaped being lynched by an enraged mob of white colonists furious that he had criticized them publicly in meetings in India—his first forays into politics were not particularly promising. The early Gandhi was still a loyal subject of the British empire, as manifest in his support of the British during the Boer War (despite his own avowed sympathies for the Boers). His methods of struggle were clearly those of the moderates in the Indian National Congress, which entailed petitioning the authorities to obtain redress, writing pamphlets full of legal arguments, and holding peaceful meetings where moderate resolutions were adopted. He was still far from being a popular leader; he pursued limited political aims which reflected the narrow social base of the movements with which he was associated. In spite of his activism and devotion to the cause of the advancement of South African Indians, he did not obtain any noticeable success in fending off a host of discriminatory legislation which gradually reduced the status of the 'Free Indians' of Natal to that of indentured coolies. His South African stay appeared to close on a note of failure in 1901 when he went back to India and appeared poised to embark upon a political career in the shadow of his political mentor, Gokhale.

His return to South Africa in 1902, at the behest of his compatriots, heralded a new phase in his career. Re-establishing himself in Durban, he embarked upon his first journalistic venture with the creation of a weekly paper entitled *Indian Opinion*, in which he started a relentless press campaign for the rights of South African Indians. In 1904, influenced by reading Ruskin, and by his advocacy of a simple life and a return to nature, he moved with a few friends and disciples to a farm in Phoenix near Durban, his first experiment in communal life. In 1905 he took his family to Johannesburg, where he opened a lawyer's office and, for the first time in his life, enjoyed a considerable measure of professional success. To all appearances he was destined for the life of the publicist more than that of the activist, but the promulgation in August 1906 of the draft of a new Transvaal Asiatic Amendments Act, which sought to impose registration and fingerprinting of all the Indians of the province, led to a spate of protests, in which Gandhi took the lead.

From 1906 onwards Gandhi entered fully into political life and enlarged his appeal to other categories of the South African Indian population, beyond the merchant élite. Between 1907 and 1913 he gradually perfected a technique of political agitation which he called *satyagraha*, to distinguish it from the term 'passive resistance', with which it was generally equated. In 1909 the first biography of Gandhi, by Reverend Joseph Doke, an English clergyman in South Africa, appeared and gave him an audience beyond South Africa, in India and Britain. Thus, at the same time as his life took a new turn, his legend was born. In 1909 he also wrote his first major political text, *Hind Swaraj*, which remained the only systematic elaboration of his political philosophy, a text in which he virulently criticized Western civilization and its effect upon India.

The 1909–19 period was a crucial phase of transition in Gandhi's life. During five years of political struggle in South Africa, culminating in the October 1913 miners' march from Natal to Transvaal—which in some ways prefigured the more famous Salt March of 1930—he refined the method of mass agitation which he later employed on such a massive scale in India. In a negotiation with Smuts, the South African premier, in July 1914, he obtained significant concessions for Indians, in particular the suppression of a vexatious tax and an acknowledgement of the validity of Hindu and Muslim marriages that had been contested by a court in 1913. His South African stay thus ended on a note of success, albeit of a limited nature.

Having gone back to India for good in 1915—after a few months' stay in London during which he helped raise an ambulance unit for the war among Indian students—he kept a low profile for some time. This was a phase of slow accumulation of forces and of learning about India, a country about which he knew so little, having spent two decades away from it. His first active intervention was in Champaran in Bihar, where he helped local peasants fight the oppression of British indigo planters. Then came a workers' strike in Ahmedabad, where he had established his ashram, in which he played the role of mediator between capital and labour. The Champaran episode, in particular, made his name familiar for the first time to the Indian masses. During these years he progressively lost his illusions about the benevolence of British rule. While in 1918 he had actively campaigned for recruitment to the Indian Army in the First World War, he became indignant at the promulgation of the Rowlatt Bills (a series of laws aimed at repressing political dissent) in March 1919. He found himself suddenly the object of public attention when he launched, almost single-handed, the Rowlatt satyagraha in April 1919. The initial response was overwhelming, but from Gandhi's point of view the movement was a failure as his calls for non-violence went unheeded and Punjab became engulfed in an orgy of arson and violence. This culminated in the Amritsar massacre, perpetrated at Jallianwala Bagh by General Dyer, who ordered his troops to fire upon a crowd of peaceful demonstrators, leaving hundreds dead. In spite of his own admission of a 'Himalayan blunder' in calling such a movement before he had devised ways of actually leading it, he became all at once a major player in Indian politics, so that, when in 1920 the Khilafat agitation—

aimed at the defence of the Califate of Islam, the existence of which was threatened by British policy towards the defunct Ottoman Empire—acquired momentum, he was in a position to mobilize the Congress Party in support of the Khilafatists. At the end of 1920 he launched the non-cooperation movement, which pursued the triple objective of defending the Khilafat, setting right the Punjab wrongs, and, for the first time, obtaining swaraj or self-rule.

From 1920 he became the leading figure of the Indian national-ist movement fighting British rule. Although the sudden end of non-cooperation in February 1922, following a massacre at Chauri-Chaura in the United Provinces of twenty-two policemen by an enraged crowd of demonstrators, left many of his supporters puzzled and unhappy, his trial by a British court and subsequent imprisonment gave him the aura of martyrdom which he always knew how to use to his advantage. In jail, he found the time to write his famous autobiography, conceived as something of a response to a book by Romain Rolland.[1] During the 1922–47 period, he alternated between phases of withdrawal and active participation in nationalist politics. When he came out of jail in 1924, he chose to devote most of his time to social reform activities, in particular to the promotion of *khadi* (handmade cloth) and the fight against untouchability. He let others conduct the day-to-day political struggle and intervened only occasionally in the life of the Congress Party.

In 1928 he came out of semi-retirement to lead once again the nationalist party as it fought for new constitutional reforms. When, in December 1929, Congress adopted as its objective complete independ-ence (Poorna Swaraj), it was left to Gandhi to define the concrete modalities of a campaign. In January 1930 he launched the call to Civil Disobedience and started the campaign with the celebrated Salt March of March–April 1930. For almost a year the Indian nationalist movement, under his guidance, and, after his imprisonment in May, that of his lieutenants, openly challenged British rule, provoking the wonder and admiration of international public opinion at the almost complete lack of violence in such a large-scale agitation. The Mahatma was then at the pinnacle of his glory and crowds literally worshipped

[1] R. Rolland, *Mahatma Gandhi*, Paris, 1924.

him. But he did not lose his *sang-froid*, and, when the opportunity arose to seek a compromise, he seized it eagerly. The pact he signed in March 1931 with the viceroy, Lord Irwin, led to the temporary suspension of Civil Disobedience and Gandhi's participation in the second Round Table Conference in London, which debated the shape of new constitutional reforms.

Having failed to obtain significant concessions from the British, Gandhi went back to India and, before he could launch a new campaign of agitation, was arrested. While the movement gradually weakened, Gandhi tried, from his jail, to dissuade the Untouchables from accepting separate electorates in the new constitution, going on a hunger strike to put pressure on the British and on the Untouchable leader Dr Bhimrao Ambedkar. Ambedkar had to give in to the intensity of popular feeling aroused by Gandhi's 'fast unto death' and sign the Poona Pact, by which he renounced separate electorates, a concession which was then accepted by London. In 1934 Gandhi officially put an end to Civil Disobedience in spite of the fact that none of its avowed objectives had been reached.

When he came out of jail Gandhi chose again not to involve himself directly in the political struggle, and, from a new ashram in Sevagram near Wardha in Central India, focused more than ever on a 'constructive programme', the fight for temple entry for Untouchables and the struggle for khadi. He also devoted a lot of attention to education as he thought the inadequacy of the existing educational system was a crucial cause of India's poverty. Although he was not openly active in politics, he retained enormous moral influence and played a crucial role in the decision, taken by the Congress in 1937, to form governments in provinces where it had gained a majority under a new constitution giving more powers to provincial governments. The compromise lasted two years, ending only with Viceroy Lord Linlithgow's unilateral decision to declare war on Germany without consulting the Legislative Assembly. The Congress answered by resigning from the provincial governments it headed.

For the following three years, Gandhi, while sticking to his view that India's participation in the war was contrary to his credo of non-violence, sought a compromise with the British and actually avoided hampering the war effort. In 1940–1 he launched a limited campaign of civil disobedience which had a weak impact, but the failure of the Cripps Mission, sent in March 1942 by the British government, to produce a compromise between London and the Congress over constitutional reforms, led him to reconsider his stance. In August 1942, while the Japanese, having overrun Burma, reached the Bengal border, he launched the 'Quit India' movement. London's reaction was swift; Gandhi was arrested, while the movement, which took a violent form, was severely repressed.

From his jail in 1943 Gandhi embarked upon a new 'fast unto death' to protest against Linlithgow's accusation that he was behind the unrest in 1942, but British intransigence forced him to call it off without having obtained an apology from the government. In 1944, Gandhi suffered a grievous blow when his wife Kasturbai, who had become a very close associate in the struggle, died. His health deteriorated, which led to his release from confinement. In September 1944 he opened direct negotiations with Jinnah to try to find a compromise between the Congress and the Muslim League over the question of Pakistan, but failed because of stubbornness on both sides. This was to be his last direct intervention in the process which led to independence and Partition.

Between 1944 and 1947 he remained largely in the background, leaving Nehru and Patel to negotiate the final agreement with the British and the Muslim League. In spite of his personal opposition to Partition, which he viewed as the negation of his entire lifework— based on the idea that differences between religions were only superficial—he chose not to oppose it. Had he chosen otherwise, it would not have made much difference; for, in spite of his enormous prestige in India and abroad, he was increasingly isolated politically. His interventions in 1946–7 were mostly geared to limiting communal violence, first in Noakhali, where he spent several weeks risking his life to help restore calm; then in Bihar, where his intervention helped put an end to massacres of Muslims; later in Calcutta where, on the eve of independence, he managed to obtain a lull in the violence which proved lasting; and finally in Delhi, where his mediation avoided further massacres at the end of 1947. Despite growing physical exhaustion, he was planning a visit to Pakistan to try to defuse tension between the two newly independent countries, but on 30 January 1948, at his daily prayer meeting held on the grounds of Birla House in New Delhi, he fell to the bullets of a Hindu extremist militant, Nathuram Godse. His earthly life ended in this brutal way, but among the mourning millions, in India and elsewhere, there also began a posthumous life which has been particularly rich and eventful.

The existing overabundant literature on Gandhi focuses mostly on his personality and his ideas at the expense of a balanced appreciation of his historical role. About Gandhi's personality, I will focus only on certain relatively unexplored areas. I will pay greater attention to his ideas, or at least to some of them inasmuch as they inspired his actions as a social reformer and political leader. Priority will be given to his role as a leader, for had he not initiated and led one of the great political movements of the twentieth century, it is most unlikely that much attention would have been paid to his ideas, some of which were extremely idiosyncratic.

PART ONE
Perceptions of Gandhi

CHAPTER 1

Images of Gandhi

One of the greatest paradoxes in relation to Gandhi is the contrast between the diversity of perceptions of him in his lifetime, and the very limited range of iconic representations retained of him by posterity. In his lifetime, Gandhi had been perceived successively and simultaneously as a Bolshevik, a fanatic, a trouble-maker, a hypocrite, an eccentric, a reactionary, a revolutionary, a saint, a renouncer, a messiah, an avatar. He was likened both to Lenin and to Jesus Christ, indicating the wide scope of representations. After his death, two views of him have become dominant: in India he is celebrated as the Father of the Nation, outside India he is remembered as an apostle of nonviolence. Such impoverishment in the range of representations is partly due to the selective way in which collective memory works, but it also owes a lot to deliberate attempts at appropriating him.

Gandhian Iconography

Prior to being made an icon after his death, even in his lifetime Gandhi was a much-represented figure. Gandhian imagery is heavily embedded in physicality. Gandhi's body, photographed a thousand times, even in death, inspired the likes of Cartier-Bresson and Margaret Bourke-White. Romain Rolland's remark, in his book published in 1923, that his body was not important for Gandhi is a typical misinterpretation. Gandhi himself gave a lot of attention to his body, not in a sensual way as source of pleasure, but as the mirror of the soul and a source of strength. Hence his almost obsessive interest in hygiene and dietetics which so astonished his contemporaries, and which is sometimes seen as a clear sign of his eccentricity. He was often perceived as physically weak, and certainly there was nothing impressive about his appearance. This is what one viceroy, Lord Reading, had to say of his first meeting with Gandhi in May 1921:

> There is nothing striking about his appearance. He came to visit me in a white dhoti and cap, woven on a spinning-wheel, with bare feet and legs, and my first impression on seeing him ushered into my room was that there was nothing to arrest attention in his appearance, and that I should have passed him by in the street without a second look at him. When he talks, the impression is different. . . .'[1]

Many were struck by the contrast between his unremarkable physical appearance and the aura around him which suggested great moral strength. His friend Henry Polak recounts that when he saw him for the first time he had the feeling he was 'faced with a moral giant, whose pellucid soul is a clear still lake in which one sees truth clearly mirrored'.[2] During his lifetime he impressed his compatriots more by his external appearance than by his speeches and writings. In India, people fought for his darshan. When he travelled by train, peasants in their millions tried to catch a glimpse of him. As soon as he alighted at a station, everyone wanted to see him and touch him. After his death, he became an icon in India: his portrait was to be found in many homes, from the richest to the poorest, and sometimes in Hindu households it stands even now on the family altar alongside various deities. Each Indian town and city has at least one statue of the Mahatma or a major road named after him. In the statues, he is not figured as national heroes are generally, in a bellicose attitude, but is almost always pictured half-naked, either spinning the wheel, or, with his pilgrim's stick, leading the Salt March. It is his status as an icon which is the main source of his fame, for relatively few in India nowadays have a clear idea of his real political role, notwithstanding all the official commemorations—such as those for the centenary of his birth in 1969 or for the fiftieth anniversary of his death in 1998—while his thought has been interpreted in so many contradictory ways that his influence is difficult to appraise.

[1] Reading to Montagu, 19 May 1921, British Library, Oriental and India Office Collections (OIOC), Reading Collection, Mss Eur.F.238/3.

[2] H.S.L. Polak, 'Saint, Patriot and Statesman', in C. Shukla (ed.), *Gandhiji as We Know Him*, Bombay, 1945, p. 45.

Outside India, one of the few places where his icon is publicly displayed is Bahia, in north-eastern Brazil, where a school of samba is known under the name of 'filhos do Gandhi'. Every year, at carnival time, thousands of men parade behind his portrait. The origins of this strange display are to be found in a dockers' strike which took place in Bahia in 1947, the year of India's independence; the strikers chose to place their movement under the patronage of the Indian leader and created a school of samba to popularize their struggle. This is a fairly unique case. Outside India, particularly in Western countries, there are few representations of Gandhi (except for a stray statue in a few large cities such as London or Paris), and there has always been more interest in his thought. In the West, the Gandhian legend has been an élite intellectual construction and has had little impact on the public at large. It is only during the last two decades, due in part to Attenborough's film *Gandhi*, that Gandhi has become an icon in Western countries too.

Gandhi and the West: The Saint and His Critiques

The legend born around Gandhi began from the early 1920s. Two Western intellectuals played a particularly important role in creating it. Romain Rolland's part is well known, although it is not easy now to fully take stock of his prominent place on the world intellectual scene. The part played by John Haynes Holmes in the spread of the Gandhian legend is little known outside the United States, but, given the particular resonance Gandhi found in that country, it deserves more attention.

These two men were not the first Westerners to have taken an interest in Gandhi. Actually the first author to have written about Gandhi was Reverend Joseph Doke, an English Baptist clergyman sympathetic to the cause of Indians in South Africa. Written in simple and accessible language, his book[3] presented the encounter of the clergyman with Gandhi as a true spiritual experience and was not short on comparing him with Jesus and Mary: 'Our Indian friend lives on a

[3] J.J. Doke, *M.K. Gandhi: An Indian Patriot in South Africa*, London, 1909 (2nd edn, New Delhi, 1967).

higher plane than most men do. His actions, like the actions of Mary of Bethany, are often counted eccentric, and not infrequently misunderstood. Those who do not know him think there is some unworthy motive behind, some Oriental "slimness" to account for such profound unworldliness. But those who know him well are ashamed of themselves in his presence.' Emphasizing how much Gandhi's absence of greed astonished and even exasperated his compatriots, Doke concluded: 'He is one of those outstanding characters with whom to walk is a liberal education, whom to know is to love.'

In his article, significantly entitled 'Saint Gandhi',[4] Mark Juergensmeyer has outlined the main stages in the growth of a 'Christian' legend around the figure of Gandhi. Overlooking Doke's contribution, he singles out Willy Pearson, an English clergyman close to C.F. Andrews, as being the first to describe Gandhi as a saint—in the manner of Saint Francis of Assisi. A decisive step in the ongoing process of canonization of Gandhi as a Christian saint was the sermon delivered in New York in April 1921 by the Unitarian pastor John Haynes Holmes, one of the figureheads of Liberal Protestantism in the United States. In his speech Holmes told a puzzled audience that the 'greatest living human being' was neither Lenin nor Romain Rolland but an obscure Indian agitator called Mohandas Karamchand Gandhi. He went on:

> In his private character, he is simple and undefiled. In his political endeavours, he is as stern a realist as Lenin, working steadfastly towards a far goal of liberation which must be won. At the same time, however, he is an idealist like Romain Rolland, living ever in the pure radiance of the spirit. When I think of Rolland . . . I think of Tolstoi. When I think of Lenin, I think of Napoleon. But when I think of Gandhi, I think of Jesus Christ. He lives his life; he speaks his word; he suffers, strives and will some day nobly die, for his kingdom upon earth.[5]

[4] M. Juergensmeyer, 'Saint Gandhi', in J. Stratton Hanley (ed.), *Saints and Virtues*, Berkeley, 1987, pp. 187–203.

[5] J.H. Holmes, 'Who is the Greatest Man in the World Today?', in H.T. Muzumdar (ed.), *The Enduring Greatness of Gandhi. An American Estimate. Being the Sermons of Dr John Haynes Holmes and Dr Donald S. Harrington*, Ahmedabad, 1982.

Holmes saw in Gandhi more than a saint, almost a saviour, a new messiah. During the rest of his life he was an active propagandist of Gandhi's ideas and of India's cause in the United States,[6] and, through his writings and sermons, helped accredit with an American public a view of Gandhi as being the modern saint. Holmes's homilies, however, had little impact outside America and Romain Rolland's intervention was needed to give the Gandhian legend its truly global dimension.

In his recent biography of the French medieval king Saint Louis, Jacques le Goff has presented him as being largely an invention of the great chronicler Joinville. In a similar way, Gandhi outside India could be said to be the invention of Romain Rolland. The essay this French writer published in 1923[7] had an enormous impact; it was translated into many languages (including several Indian languages) and went through several reprints. Romain Rolland's prestige was then at its peak: his critical attitude towards the great butchery of 1914–18 had elevated him to the status of keeper of the conscience of the world, in the manner of Tolstoi prior to the Great War. What he wrote carried a lot of weight with intellectuals worldwide. Many years later, Rolland explained how and why he was attracted to Gandhi:

> To the fountains of somnambulant India, I had not come to nurture only a cosmic dream; I had brought there my European preoccupations, the spectre of the war which had raged over Western fields and which was still prowling around the ossuaries. I knew only too well that the Erynnies were hiding near the tombs from which arose the smoke of shed blood. And I felt an anxious desire to raise against them . . . a rampart of sovereign reason, able to put an end to conflict. There was nothing to expect from the triumphant Western imperialisms who were intent on enjoying the spoils and, in their stupid state of bloated satisfaction, were not even cautious enough to properly keep watch on those spoils. I thought I had found that rampart in the revelation given to me in 1922 of the little Saint Francis of India, Gandhi. Did he bring, in the folds of his sackcloth, the word which would free us of the murders to come, the heroic non-violence

---

[6] See L. Gordon, 'Mahatma Gandhi's Dialogues with Americans', *Economic and Political Weekly*, vol.XXXVII, no. 4, 26 January–1 February 2002, pp. 337–52.

[7] R. Rolland, *Mahatma Gandhi*, op. cit.

which does not flee, but resists, 'Ahimsa'? I had such need to believe in it that I believed in it passionately for many years, and I poured out that faith in full buckets. I was convinced (I confess it) that it alone could bring salvation to a crime-ridden world, its past crimes, its future crimes.

Rolland's book on Gandhi is actually full of errors and approximations, reflecting second-hand knowledge and a lack of familiarity with the Indian context, but the combination of deep empathy and literary skill explains why the text had such an impact and helped to make Gandhi a well-known figure beyond India and the English-speaking countries.

It is worth quoting the first few lines of the text, they give a good idea of Rolland's tone:

> Quiet dark eyes. A small, weak man, with a thin face and big ears. Wearing a white cap as headgear, clothed in rough white material, barefoot. He feeds on rice and fruits, drinks only water, sleeps on the floor, rests little, works all the time. Nothing about him strikes more than an expression of great patience and great love. Pearson, who saw him in 1913 in South Africa, was reminded of Francis of Assisi. He is simple like a child, soft and polite even with his adversaries, immaculately sincere . . . never hides his mistakes, never makes compromises, has no diplomacy, hates eloquence, or, even better, does not think of it; shrinks from the popular demonstrations which his presence suscitates . . . literally sick of the adoring multitude; fundamentally distrustful of numbers and averse to Mobocracy, to the reign of the populace; he feels at ease only in the minority, happy only in solitude, listening to the still small voice as it commands . . . Such is the man who has incited to revolt three hundred million men, has shaken the British Empire and launched the most powerful movement in the politics of mankind for almost two thousand years.

In this text Rolland played on several binary oppositions—between physical weakness and moral strength, popular adulation and taste for solitude—to draw a picture of Gandhi as embodying Christlike or Franciscan simplicity, in total contrast to the conventional Western view of an 'Oriental'. The secret of the fascination held by Gandhi over many Westerners lay precisely in this contrast: they felt that, behind his apparent otherness, he was actually a figure of sameness.

The picture of Gandhi drawn by Rolland, for a European public totally ignorant about him, relied on both proximity and aloofness. He started with what was most foreign, Gandhi's Hinduism. Emphasizing the crucial role of religion in his make-up, he took care to stress that 'Gandhi believes strongly in the religion of his people, Hinduism', but immediately qualified this statement by reducing Gandhi's Hinduism to a variety of Christianity. While recognizing Gandhi's belief in sacred cows and the caste system, he attempted to show that his ultimate inspiration was Christian. He discerned, 'under the cloth of the Hindu credo [sic]', 'the great evangelic heart', and saw in Gandhi 'a more tender, more appeased, and more Christian Tolstoi, in the universal sense', for Tolstoi, according to him, was Christian less by nature than by will. He perceived Tolstoi's influence in Gandhi's condemnation of modern civilization, which he took rather literally as 'a negation of progress and European science', while noting also that Gandhi was ready to make realistic compromises with the modern world. He quoted Gandhi's definition of himself as a 'practical idealist' and stressed the deep relationship he had developed with the Indian people. He then presented a detailed account of Gandhi's struggle between 1919 and 1922. His conclusion was an attempt at enlarging the meaning of the Gandhian message:

> Our non-violence is the fiercest struggle. The path to peace is not through weakness. We detest violence less than weakness. There is nothing to be gained without strength, neither good, nor evil. And better evil in its entirety than emasculated good. Whining pacifism is fatal to peace: it is cowardly and faithless. Let those who do not believe or are afraid withdraw! The path to peace is through self-sacrifice. This is Gandhi's lesson. Only the Cross is missing.

Rolland's most important contribution to the birth of the Gandhian legend was the link he established between the European intelligentsia's preoccupation with peace and Gandhi's teaching, a link which was not self-evident. He made Gandhi into more than the leader of a national liberation movement, that being the way in which Gandhi was generally perceived. At the same time, Rolland did not particularly seek to make him into a saint, for he wanted to present him as an example, and saints do not make good examples. He tried to construct him as a modern hero who was showing the way to mankind. Rolland's own prestige gave particular credibility to his statement of the universal character of Gandhi's message. He freed Gandhi from everyday politics and journalism to give him a degree of permanence, and sought to transform him from an Indian into a global figure. Largely thanks to Rolland, Gandhi escaped oblivion once the curtain had fallen on non-cooperation. Rolland's reconstruction of Gandhi did not owe everything to the writer's imagination: although he had not met Gandhi (their actual meeting took place at Rolland's place in Switzerland in 1931), and had never been to India, he used all the available evidence to him to draw his picture. The end result was the creation of an archetype.

In spite of Rolland's efforts to make Gandhi accessible to a Western public without falling into simplistic hagiography, the dominant perception of the Mahatma in Christian circles, which were the most responsive to his message, was that of a saint, or of a Christ-like figure. Gandhi's sartorial simplicity was one of the features which assimilated him to the Messiah in the eyes of an audience steeped in biblical references. The notion of Gandhi's saintly character spread throughout Anglo-Saxon Protestant Christendom, most particularly in the United States. In Lutheran and Catholic circles it was much less widely accepted, even if Gandhi acquired followers with a Catholic background such as Jean-Joseph Lanza del Vasto, the Frenchman of Italian origin who was the main propagator of Gandhism in France. The Catholic Church is not in the habit of recognizing non-Catholic saints, and the Mahatma's Catholic admirers tended as a rule to be somewhat marginal *vis-à-vis* the Church. It must be recalled in particular that, on the occasion of Gandhi's visit to Rome in 1931 (which was exploited by Mussolini's propaganda), Pope Pius XI refused to receive him in the Vatican.

Gandhi's 'christianization' actually rested upon some cultural misunderstanding: the 'polysemic' nature of perceptions of Gandhi in India offers a striking contrast to the reductionism implied in his transformation into a Christian saint, given the poverty of the symbolic register of Christian saintliness, especially its Protestant version. And yet it set an indelible mark on Western views of Gandhi and, as a result, had some influence on Indian perceptions of the Mahatma.

There remained always a certain degree of ambiguity in the relationship between Gandhi and his Christian admirers. Gandhi did nothing to incite them to elevate him to sainthood, but he was shrewd enough politically to understand all the advantages he could derive from being put on such a pedestal. Actually, as Juergensmeyer rightly argues, the canonization of Gandhi had more to do with the problems of some Christian intellectuals *vis-à-vis* the modern world than with Gandhi's personality or his actions. Gandhi's saintliness was largely a proxy saintliness into which some Western Christian intellectuals projected their own frustrations and expectations.

In his lifetime Gandhi was not viewed as a saint by the Western public at large. In England, where he naturally aroused more interest than anywhere else, opinions were fairly divided. His admirers were found mostly among Quakers and more generally Protestant religious circles. He also drew support from some prominent intellectuals, such as George Bernard Shaw, but on the whole did not have much impact on artistic and literary milieux. George Orwell, writing about him in 1949,[8] confessed that, for a long period, he had little interest in his ideas. The popular press was generally hostile to him. But, during his visit in 1931 at the time of the Round Table Conference, he did arouse some popular acclaim. In London's East End, where he established his residence, he was on the whole well received.

His visit to Lancashire, in spite of the fact that his call to boycott British cloth had hit the local mills, was quasi-triumphal. In popular reactions, curiosity towards an 'exotic' character played a big part. In political circles, though he evoked a more positive response from Labour than Tory supporters, even those who tended to be sympathetic to Indian aspirations found his ideas somewhat strange. British rulers, irrespective of party affiliation, saw in him a tricky opponent and often hesitated about the best way to deal with him. Among British viceroys, who were confronted with him between 1920 and 1947, different strands of opinion are discernible. Men such as Lord Reading, himself a British Jew with an atypical trajectory, or Lord Irwin, a representative of high anglicanism, showed themselves sensitive to his spiritual dimension and expressed some sympathy for him, generally mixed with a degree of exasperation. Reading wrote in 1924 to King George V: 'I prefer him . . . to any of the others, for although he

[8] G. Orwell, 'Reflections on Gandhi', *Partisan Review*, 16 January 1949, pp. 85–92. It was only after having read the *Autobiography* that Orwell became convinced of Gandhi's greatness.

is a visionary, and I do not accept literally everything he says, yet he has sincere convictions and is on the high ethical plane so long as he keeps away from politics'.[9] Irwin, for his part, recognized the sincerity of his convictions and advised treating him with the consideration due to one with immense moral stature. On the other hand two later viceroys, Linlithgow and Wavell, who were more conformist and less religiously inclined, did not hesitate to call him a hypocrite and expressed feelings of hostility towards him. His British interlocutors were often unsettled by the contrast between his mastery of the English language and what they saw as his affectation in disguising himself as an Indian peasant. Churchill's well-known broadside against Gandhi as a Middle Temple lawyer parading in the guise of a 'naked fakir'[10] (which was in fact directed as much at Irwin, accused of treating on an equal footing a simple agitator) is typical of the kind of exasperation aroused among members of the British ruling class by his style of dress, which they saw as contrary to good taste and decency. On the other hand, it was precisely the meagreness of his clothing which contributed, in the eyes of many, to his saintly image.

While there were strong reservations about Gandhi in many circles throughout the 1920s and 1930s, this did not prevent a growing wave of admiration. When in 1939 the philosopher Sarvepalli Radhakrishnan edited a volume in homage to Gandhi for his seventieth birthday,[11] all the authors, which included prestigious figures such as Einstein, Arnold Zweig and Salvador de Madariaga, agreed he was the greatest man of the century. From 1937 onwards, he was regularly mentioned in relation to the Nobel Peace Prize, and only the Eurocentrism of the Norwegian committee deprived him of an award many thought he

[9] Reading to King George V, 10 September 1924, Reading Collection, Mss Eur. F. 238 /1.

[10] 'It is alarming and also nauseating to see Mr Gandhi, a seditious Middle Temple lawyer, now posing as a fakir of a type well known in the East, striding half-naked up the steps of the Viceregal Palace, while he is still organizing and conducting a defiant campaign of civil disobedience, to parley on equal terms with the representative of the King-Emperor.' Quoted in G. Ashe, *Gandhi: A Study in Revolution*, London, 1968, p. XI.

[11] S. Radhakrishnan (ed.), *Mahatma Gandhi: Essays and Reflections on His Life and Work*, London, 1939.

deserved. Admiration was not however unanimous and in some Western countries such as France, Gandhi's greatness was recognized only after his death.

Gandhi's Image in France

On the reception given to Gandhi in France, a recent study provides interesting insights.[12] It is only belatedly that Gandhi drew the attention of the popular press. During the 1920s, most notices of him came from a few Catholic and pacifist intellectuals who wrote in rather confidential journals. The well-known Islamologist Louis Massignon discovered him as early as 1920 through his Indian Muslim contacts and published a translation of one of his speeches in the *Revue du Monde Musulman* in 1922. This text was used later by the Catholic philosopher Jacques Maritain. Massignon appears to have found some resemblance between Gandhi and the Muslim mystic al-Hallaj, on whom he had worked, and seen in him a figure transcending religious boundaries: this drew the attention of some Catholic intellectuals. Romain Rolland's role in introducing Gandhi to the French has already been underlined, but his exile to Switzerland had estranged him from the mainstream of French intellectual life and he did not really succeed in infecting the Parisian intelligentsia with his enthusiasm for Gandhi.

During the 1920s it seems that two very different perceptions of Gandhi coexisted. For some, the Mahatma was an anti-imperialist revolutionary: in an article in *Clarté* in 1923, Henri Barbusse, then France's most prominent Communist intellectual, explicitly likened him to Lenin and praised him for having inspired the Indian masses with a spirit of resistance akin to that injected into the Russian masses by the Bolshevik leader. Henri Massis, a prominent member of the monarchist Action Française, denounced him in 1927, in his *Défense de l'Occident,* as an enemy of Western Christian civilization, but thought his star was on the decline as his doctrine was losing ground to communism. It may appear strange to us, but drawing a

[12] M.F. Latronche, *L'influence de Gandhi en France de 1919 à nos jours*, Paris, 1999.

parallel between Gandhi and Lenin seems to have been a widespread exercise in the 1920s, reflecting the fact that both men were widely perceived as anti-imperialist revolutionaries who provoked enthusiasm as well as fear in different quarters. Some were, however, more alert to Gandhi's spiritual dimension, and his message of non-violence struck a chord with a fraction of Catholic intellectuals, including those who were close to Marc Sangnier and his movement 'Le Sillon'. Civil Disobedience and the Salt March inspired renewed interest in Gandhi, and the Parisian press gave extended coverage to these events. Appreciations of Gandhi's role were nevertheless rarely on the positive side: the right-wing press was blinded by its anglophilia and its colonialism, while Communists saw in Civil Disobedience a diversion playing into the hands of imperialism. A book written in the early 1930s by the famous journalist Andrée Viollis, *L'Inde contre les Anglais*, did much to make him better known to the French public.

During his only visit to France, which took place in December 1931, when he was on his way back to India from attending the Round Table Conference in London, he aroused some curiosity in the public. A reliable witness to this period, the leftist journalist Daniel Guérin, wrote, somewhat ironically in *La Révolution Prolétarienne* (a small but fairly influential paper):

> Gandhi is a particular attraction in the aftermath of the colonial exhibition: have not newspapers, newsreels and reviewers drawn attention to his bare head, his toothless mouth and his strange white woollen cloth? The fast train comes into the station. There is a rush towards his car. And the diminutive and frail old man makes his appearance, with his brown face, his impassive look, and is immediately surrounded and crushed by a crowd which pushes him towards the exit as if he were straw in the wind.

The same evening Gandhi held a meeting at the Magic Circus, a popular sports arena, which drew a substantial crowd. The Paris newspapers commented this in a decidedly malevolent tone. While the communist newpaper *l'Humanité* ranted against the 'traitor Gandhi', whom it accused of perpetrating a 'fraudulent political act', and dismissed his speech as 'utter rubbish', Gaëtan Sanvoisin of the right-wing *Le Figaro* was barely less agressive, with his talk of 'laughable truisms' and his accusation that Gandhi was an agent of pacifism.

Venomous hostility reached a new height in an article written by the well-known right-wing journalist and writer Georges Suarez in *L'Echo de Paris* under the significant heading: 'A première at Magic-City: Mahatma Gandhi proves himself to be a great comic'. Suarez wrote: 'It cannot be said that Mahatma Gandhi exudes a victorious air. He appears crushed by his lamentable half-nakedness. He has been clothed in the garb of a messiah or a conqueror; but, if his sandals are those of Mahomet, his little bathing-suit does not bring to mind the frock coat Napoléon wore in Wagram . . .' He ended with the following sentence: 'after a few banalities on the Anglo-Hindu [*sic*] conflict, the curtain fell on the fakir'. Another right-wing paper, *le Temps*, was more moderate in its comments but castigated the 'half-circus, half-dancing-hall' atmosphere reigning at the meeting to conclude that Gandhi was out of place in front of a Parisian audience.

Reading through the Parisian press of the period, one is made aware of how ill-informed French opinion was about events in India and how dismissive journalists were of a leader who had already acquired an international stature. Inter-imperialist solidarity is probably the key to the attitude of the right-wing press: right-wingers were afraid of a possible spread of anti-colonial agitation from India to French colonies (there was an anti-French rising in Indochina in 1931), and besides, there was considerable ignorance of the Indian context, even in 'enlightened' circles. The dominant image of Gandhi carried by the press was of a trouble-maker, of a hypocrite, certainly not of a saint.

His visit however had some positive consequences: an association of the Friends of Gandhi was created by Louise Guyiesse and, from 1932 onwards, it published a bulletin, *Nouvelles de l'Inde*, which had a very small circulation. The tiny group of his French admirers, amongst whom Louis Massignon remained active till the end of his life, succeeded in enlarging the appeal of his ideas beyond the small circles which closely followed Indian affairs. In the review *Esprit*, an influential voice of progressive Catholicism, Emmanuel Mounier wrote several articles in which he showed an interest in Gandhi's theory and practice of non-violence. His ideas of course appealed particularly to pacifists, who were prone as a rule to misinterpret the meaning of Gandhian non-violence. While Socialists tended to support his actions to a degree, Communists remained hostile to him till the end, even if they avoided the extreme attacks of their ultra-sectarian phase. His main disciple in France, Lanza del Vasto, always remained a somewhat marginal figure in the political and intellectual landscape, although his *Pèlerinage aux sources*,[13] which narrated his encounter with Gandhi in India in 1936, sold 200,000 copies at the time of the German occupation of France—a very high figure indeed for the period. Its success can probably be explained by the specific circumstances of the times: the French were in search of diversions to help them forget their miseries, and India held a lot of attraction. Besides, among some at least, Gandhi could be construed as preaching a return to the land, in the manner of the Vichy régime.

It is only towards the end of Gandhi's life, when his political role was on the wane, that he became a figure of veneration in France, his tragic death definitely giving him the aura of a martyr. *Le Monde* then wrote: 'The death of the champion of Indian independence will deeply move public opinion, which will deplore the demise of one of the last and most authentic witnesses for peace, at the time when he had just obtained his greatest victory.' Among France's statesmen, the Gaullist Maurice Schumann (who met him a few days before his death in his capacity as head of a French mission to the new Indian authorities) was probably the most eloquent in his praise: 'This tragic news . . . is felt by me as a personal bereavement. Since the moment when I was lucky enough to approach this great man, I think of him daily as one of the rare witnesses to the unity of mankind in a torn, harassed, soulless world.' He added: 'France has lost a precious friend at the same time as India has lost an irreplaceable guide.' In the French Chambre des Députés, MPs observed a minute's silence in homage (with the exception of the Communists). In a more confidential meeting of his French disciples, Lanza del Vasto tried to control his emotions and find in the tragedy ground for hope:

> Let us not cry, my friends. Let us be full of joy. He came out of the changing days to enter eternity. Let us envy him rather . . . I believe since Jesus Christ such an example had not been seen. He was a saint, a sage, a master and a hero. He died of violent death, as fits a man of non-violence. Of him I keep a white memory . . . I lost my father. But Gandhi is not dead, he will never die.

[13] J.J. Lanza del Vasto, *Pèlerinage aux Sources*, Paris, 1943.

An even cursory evocation of the French case shows how wide the contrast is between perceptions of Gandhi when he was alive, which were far from unanimously favourable, and the universal veneration which has reigned after his death. This is an example of transfiguration quite unique in the twentieth century. No 'revisionism' has manifested itself in relation to Gandhi in the fifty years after his death, even if the admiration of posterity has sometimes been watered down. The advent in 1982 of Attenborough's film *Gandhi* certainly helped make him an international icon.

Gandhi on the Screen: Consecration of the Icon

Richard Attenborough's *Gandhi* gave a major boost to the Gandhian legend in the West. It is curious that no significant film on Gandhi was made before the 1980s; one might also wonder why the best-known film was made by a Western rather than an Indian film-maker, considering that India has no dearth of cinematographic talent. Perhaps Gandhi is a controversial topic in India and studio proprietors prefer to avoid controversy.

Attenborough's script was based on a biography of Gandhi by Louis Fischer,[14] a well-known American journalist who had been a Communist sympathizer and had fallen under the spell of the Mahatma in the late 1930s. Leaving aside the question of cinematographic quality, which is irrelevant here, it must be admitted that the film is not devoid of emotional appeal and, more importantly, constitutes a very faithful summary of the Gandhian legend as it is perceived in the West. In his film, Attenborough chose parable over epic, and this choice of narrative strategy is significant, reflecting the strong parallel between the lives of Gandhi and Jesus Christ which runs throughout the film as an implicit theme. The narrative progression is through a succession of episodes which illustrate Gandhi's march towards triumph and martyrdom. The film opens with Gandhi's assassination and his funerals, and that sequence is followed by a flashback to the time of Gandhi's arrival in South Africa in 1893. There is nothing on his childhood and youth.

[14] L. Fischer, *The Life of Mahatma Gandhi*, New York, 1950.

Gandhi arriving in South Africa and being brutally expelled from a first-class compartment on a train is not exactly the young man one would expect to see. Although his European clothes and way of speaking reveal the lawyer just out of law school, there is already in him a kind of inner light which singles him out as a man of destiny. There is a deliberate attempt at iconizing him, this being helped by the actor Ben Kingsley's remarkable interpretation. The film presents an essentialist vision of Gandhi: the young lawyer who has just landed in South Africa diffuses that halo of saintliness which will later radiate from the Mahatma. Essence foregrounds existence, to use Sartre's categories. Although the narrative is quite discontinuous, Gandhi's progress is shown as marked by a great degree of continuity, each episode suggesting enrichment and the inexorable march of fate.

Gandhi's saintliness in the film is, however, quite different from the kind conferrred on him by the likes of Holmes, who saw him as a messianic figure. The sanctity is mostly related to his capacity to embody individual consciousness as it battles oppressive forces, be this the racism of the whites in South Africa or the arrogant imperialism of the British epitomised by the infamous Amritsar massacre of 1919—a central episode in the film—although Gandhi was not directly involved here. Gandhi's saintly character is thus resolutely modern and individualistic, and the religious aspect is subsidiary. Actually the film is very discreet about Gandhi's religious convictions, and in particular the nature of his Hinduism. It does not paint him as a Christian or crypto-Christian, yet a certain ambiguity remains. The explanation for this cautious approach is probably in terms of the Western audience targeted: the aim of the film is to show the modernity and continuing relevance of Gandhi, while to a Western audience Hinduism often appears archaic, if not obscurantist. In order to become a modern saint accessible to a Western audience, Gandhi had to be 'dehinduized'. Although the film has not been unanimously acclaimed in the West,[15] it has shaped to a large extent popular perceptions of the Mahatma. In India, where reception of the film has been more mixed, but attendance enormous, intellectual circles have criticized Attenborough for transforming Gandhi into an icon for Westerners and for simplifying a very complex character.

[15] See the severe criticism of the film by Michael Edwardes, in M. Edwardes, *The Myth of the Mahatma: Gandhi, the British and the Raj*, London, 1986.

Gandhi in Indian Eyes: Diversity of Perceptions and Practices

Gandhi's unique place in modern India's imagination, despite the scarcity of cinematographic representations, is best conveyed by a study of his image in modern literature, in English as well as in Indian languages, which is outside the scope of this book. As early as 1921 he inspired Hindi literature's most celebrated author, Premchand. In the latter's novel *Premashram* (The Ashram of Love), focused around agrarian conflict in an Indian village, the central character, Premsankar, is an obvious alias of Gandhi. Apart from novelists, Gandhi inspired dramatists, and several plays have taken as their subject episodes of his life. The appellation 'Mahatma', or 'great soul', which is said to have been conferred on him by Rabindranath Tagore in 1915, well expressed the veneration with which he was held by his countrymen. In his own circle of friends and acquaintances he was generally called Bapu, father, which had a different connotation. His public dialogue, sometimes conflictual, with the great Bengali poet,[16] is a clear indication of the impact he had upon the intelligentsia. But more importantly, from 1920 Gandhi gathered nationwide appeal, the first such occurrence for an individual in India, earlier leaders having been regional heroes. Perceptions of him varied enormously through the country, but with Civil Disobedience in 1930 he started being transformed into the dominant symbol of Indian nationalism. Views of him remained somewhat unfixed, all the same, until his assassination made him the national hero and the object of an official cult.

Gandhi's 'polysemy' in his lifetime was linked to his broad symbolic register, which left him open to different kinds of interpretation. Gandhi himself was very good at using symbols: he did not leave anything to chance, to improvisation; each of his gestures and postures was geared towards carrying across a message to different kinds of recipients. The Indian public, mostly illiterate and steeped in a culture which was predominantly oral and visual, responded very well to this use of symbols, even though this did not prevent misunderstandings, especially in relation to Gandhi's clothes.

---

[16] On the relationship between Gandhi and Tagore, see S. Bhattacharya (ed.), *The Mahatma and the Poet. Letters and Debates between Gandhi and Tagore 1915–1941*, New Delhi, 1997.

Clothes, and more generally external appearance, are important questions to consider in appraising Gandhi's personality and the ways in which he was seen by his contemporaries and posterity. To reach the illiterate masses, the Gandhian message had to be conveyed through images more than words, all the more so as—and all testimonies on this point concur—Gandhi was no great orator. The external appearance of the mature Gandhi, so idiosyncratic in the Indian context of the time, was the result of a continuous and deliberate process of self-definition and construction. In a recent book[17] the British anthropologist Emma Tarlo has drawn attention to its genesis. Gandhi appears to have been sensitive, at an early stage in his life, to the close links which existed in India between clothes, national identity and social status. From the time of his departure for England he seems to have been possessed by a 'sartorial anxiety' which can be read as a reflection of a more existential anxiety. It has already been mentioned that he tried at first to become a perfect dandy. He then adopted a standard Western style of dress, to which he remained faithful throughout his South African stay. He appeared in public in Indian dress for the first time in Durban in 1913 during a meeting. As a mark of mourning for the Indian miners killed during the satyagraha, he presented himself, head shaven, dressed only in a *lungi* and a *kurta*. In that particular case, the adoption of Indian dress was a manifestation of grief, not a triumphal affirmation, and Gandhi had not yet made definite choices. On his return to India in 1915, at first he adopted the peasant costume of Kathiawar, his native land, which tended to shock Indian political circles used to more sober styles. For a few years he tried different kinds of dress and headgear. It is during these years that he popularized a Kashmiri headgear, made of white khadi, which, under the name of 'Gandhi cap', spread throughout India to become a symbol of nationalism—which it has remained to this day.

Gandhi's main preoccupation was the promotion of khadi, which he wanted the entire population to adopt. It was an essential part of the non-cooperation programme of 1920–2 and was directly linked to the boycott of foreign cloth. But the campaign for khadi failed to make a significant impact, and it is in recognition of this fact that, at the end

[17] E. Tarlo, *Clothing Matters. Dress and Identity in India*, London, 1996.

of 1921, Gandhi decided to wear only a loincloth. As pointed out by Tarlo, this decision had nothing to do with either a desire to emphasize the 'dignity of poverty' or the greatness of Indian civilization. It was actually a kind of manifestation of mourning: as long as the poorest Indians were not able to use khadi, Gandhi would wear only minimal clothing out of solidarity with them. His aim was to incite his country-men to reject foreign cloth without being ashamed of going about half-naked; in the long term he wanted to help the development of hand-spinning and hand-weaving; for him it was an integral part of India's fight to recover its dignity. In Gandhi's mind the loincloth was a sym-bol of India's poverty which it could escape only through the adoption of khadi and the rejection of machine-made cloth. Through his own semi-nakedness he was trying to put across a message of self-suffi-ciency and emancipation from British domination, and not, as some thought, to glorify poverty. At the outset, Gandhi thought of the loincloth as a temporary measure, but he actually never went back on it. In 1931 he even appeared at an official reception at Buckingham Palace wearing it (and a woollen shawl), to the horror of British proto-col.

Although many saw in the adoption of this austere style of dressing a manifestation of Gandhi's saintliness, he always opposed this inter-pretation. For him there was no religious symbolism involved in the wearing of a loincloth, only a call to Indians to start spinning and weaving so that the poor could be decently clothed. The image of him-self that Gandhi attempted to project was very much a constructed one; it did not fit within any existing tradition and was in fact a typical example of the 'invention of tradition' which characterized all nation-alist movements in the twentieth century. Gandhi's appearance had as little to do with that of the Indian peasant (if such an ideal type could be said to have existed) as Mao's costume with Chinese peasant dress.

In spite of denials to the contrary, it is possible that Gandhi was sensitive to a certain equation between simplicity and saintliness, which represents a point of convergence between Western and Indian notions, but was probably more striking to the Western imagination, fed on images of Christ and Saint Francis of Assisi, than to the Indian. Actually, in the Indian context, other markers are more important than simplicity of dress. According to Juergensmeyer, Gandhi did not particularly fit the model of Hindu saintliness. His admirers preferred to stress his moral qualities rather than his powers or asceticism. There was, however, a difference between his perception by the élites and by the masses.

By playing upon a very varied symbolic register, Gandhi was able to establish with the Indian public a rapport of profound complicity which often escaped the eye of the British, who were not very sensitive to the nuances of Gandhian symbolism. With regard to his Indian audience, Gandhi relied a great deal on his image as a renouncer, a *sanyasi*, the sort of person who has often played an important role in religious revival and social reform movements. The clearest sign that Gandhi was a renouncer was his adoption of *brahmacharya*, from 1906. It carried considerable symbolic significance and put him on a higher plane than other political figures. Gandhi not only renounced sexuality, he also renounced family life, choosing to live in an ashram, where material resources were pooled, and where all tasks, including the humblest and most polluting (such as cleaning latrines) were performed by all. Compared to this, his simplicity of dress was a secondary marker, and one which was more calculatedly political.

Although Gandhi was seen as having renounced material goods, he was not necessarily considered otherworldly. To be a renouncer in India is a specific mode of being in the world: unlike Christianity, there is not in Hinduism a radical divide between worldliness and otherworldliness. Gandhi, despite being a renouncer, was actually considered a social and religious reformer—in the manner of Ramakrishna or Vivekananda—as much, or even more than as a political leader. As a reformer, he could not be easily labelled. He was radical in some ways, such as in his implacable hostility to untouchability, which set him apart from most Hindus, who saw it as part of Hinduism and the caste system and which earned him the hostility of some traditionalist Hindu groups. His views on the position of women in society and child marriage (which he opposed) were also fairly advanced, but his opposition to widow remarriage left him open to criticism from within the ranks of reformers. His refusal to condemn the worship of idols and his particular veneration for sacred cows were aspects of his faith which made him close to mainstream Hinduism. Although there was a certain degree of consensus about his double nature as renouncer and reformer, his ideas, as well as his way of life and external appearance, drew very different reactions from different groups in society.

Merchant communities, essentially the powerful Hindu merchant communities, which had been subjected to various reformist influences since the late nineteenth century, responded very positively to his message. Apart from being sympathetic to some of his religious views, merchants saw in him a man of their caste who understood their problems. Gandhi himself, a bania by caste who did not belong to a family of traders, was always careful to cultivate the merchant milieu from the time of his South African stay. His political style, a mixture of high spirituality and down-to-earth pragmatism, found particular resonance with merchants. They also appreciated Gandhi's open opposition to class struggle and his plea for cooperation between capital and labour.

On the other hand, those Indians who belonged to the Anglicized middle class, lawyers, doctors and other professionals who constituted the main social base of the Congress before 1920, were much less enthusiastic. As Lala Lajpat Rai said, 'Such of his countrymen as have drunk deep from the fountains of European history and European politics and who have developed a deep love for European manners and European culture, neither understand nor like him. In their eyes he is a barbarian, a visionary and a dreamer.'[18] They found him too radically anti-British and resented his taste for material simplicity, which they often saw as a manifestation of hypocrisy. They also found him too indulgent towards what they thought were popular superstitions. Mohammed Ali Jinnah, the most typical of Anglicized Indians before he became the leader of the Muslim League, expressed from 1915 onwards a deep hostility to Gandhi which was to remain till the end of their respective lives.

Gandhi's rise to the leadership of the Congress in 1920 signalled a change in the balance of forces within the political class; the Anglicized élite of the great metropolitan cities, which dominated nationalist politics prior to 1914, had been partly displaced by the rise of a new class of merchants and lawyers, some of whom hailed from smaller

[18] Quoted in Raghavan Iyer, *The Moral and Political Thought of Mahatma Gandhi*, New York, 1973.

cities and towns and were prone to express themselves in the vernacular rather than in English. This non-metropolitan middle class, which had close links with the countryside, was better placed to draw rural India into the struggle, thanks to its contacts with an upper strata of relatively rich peasants. Not all members of this class, however, rallied to Gandhi. For it is from among such middle classes in these medium-sized and small urban centres that there arose, in the 1920s, Hindu nationalist organizations such as the Hindu Mahasabha and the Rashtriya Swayamsevak Sangh (RSS), which often opposed Gandhi, accusing him of being too soft on Muslims. They held Gandhi responsible for Partition, which was paradoxical as he had always opposed it, and Gandhi's assassin Nathuram Godse used that argument as his justification. In his declaration to the court, published as a book in the 1970s[19]—a book which has incidentally been widely diffused, as Gandhi's killer has become, for some extremist milieux, a kind of cult figure—he lashed out at Gandhi's view of Muslims. His criticism developed into an all-out attack against the Mahatma, whom he accused of being incoherent and of having weakened India by his policy of non-violence.

The reaction to Gandhi in India during his lifetime was thus far from unanimously favourable. Two aspects deserve special notice. First, his ideas were received with less sympathy among Muslims than among Hindus. Gandhi came from a Hindu background which had been in close contact with Islam for centuries. His own mother's family belonged to a small syncretic sect which considered the Holy Koran a sacred book. His own conception of Indian nationalism was always inclusive of Muslims; in South Africa he had forged close links with Muslim merchants and always associated them with his struggles. And yet his popularity with the Muslim élites as well as the masses was never comparable to the one he enjoyed among Hindus.

Second, there were regional variations in the reception of the Gandhian message. His impact was particularly strong in his native Gujarat, while two regions were considerably lukewarm to Gandhi and his ideas, namely Maharashtra and Bengal. In those two provinces, the original birthplaces of Indian nationalism, nostalgia for their early

---

[19] N. Godse, *Why I Assassinated Mahatma Gandhi*, Delhi, 1993 (first published as *May It Please Your Honour*, Delhi, 1977).

dominance, along with social prejudices among a section of the élite, limited Gandhi's appeal. Nevertheless, Gandhi was the first Indian nationalist political leader who had support across the entire country, and it was one of the main reasons for his success.

In spite of his immense prestige with the masses, Gandhi met with vigorous opposition from some political circles. Apart from the Hindu nationalists, leftist circles denounced him with something approaching ferocity. He was labellled a supporter of capitalism and a stooge of imperialism, accusations which never worried him unduly. Rajani Palme Dutt formulated the communist critique of Gandhi with great eloquence and talent in *India Today*. He described him as

> the ascetic defender of property in the name of the most religious and idealist principles of humility and love of poverty; the invincible metaphysicaltheological casuist who could justify anything and everything in an astounding tangle of explanations and arguments which in a man of common clay might have been called dishonest quibbling, but in the great ones of the earth like MacDonald or Gandhi is recognized as a higher plane of spiritual reasoning; the prophet who by his personal saintliness and selflessness could unlock the door to the hearts of the masses where the moderate bourgeois could not hope for a hearing—and the best guarantee of the shipwreck of any mass movement which had the blessing of his association. . . .[20]

This severe indictment, in which a degree of admiration is also discernible, is significant of the exasperation provoked by Gandhi among a political minority which, although it thought it was equipped with an infallible political theory, could not get a hearing among the masses, the very people whom Gandhi knew how to address.

It is interesting to note that, in present-day India, Communists, who are still a political force to be reckoned with, hold a completely different view of Gandhi, whom they now recognize as the leader of the freedom struggle. A book by E.M.S. Namboodiripad published in 1959,[21] while maintaining a critical distance from Gandhi, acknowledged his positive contribution to India's freedom. Strong opposition also came from the political representatives of the Untouchables,

[20] R.P. Dutt, *India Today*, Bombay, 1940.
[21] E.M.S. Namboodiripad, *Gandhi and the 'Ism'*, Delhi, 1959 (1st edn).

particularly B.R. Ambedkar, who never forgave Gandhi for having forced his hand in 1932 on the question of separate electorates by using the weapon of 'fast unto death' which Ambedkar, not without reason, considered a form of blackmail. In a pamphlet published in 1945,[22] Ambedkar launched a violent attack against Gandhi, whom he called a 'fanatical Hindu'. The Muslim League also, under Jinnah's leadership, criticized him severely after 1934 and described him as a Hindu leader.

We have considered the attitude of leaders and political élites to Gandhi. But his greatest political contribution is recognized to have been his ability to mobilize, for the first time, broader masses, in particular the peasantry. How did the masses view him? This is not an easy question to answer, given the fact that illiterate masses leave few traces of their views. However, some historians have come up with interesting findings. Jacques Pouchepadass, in his study of peasant mobilization in the Champaran satyagraha of 1917,[23] has shown how Gandhi, from the time of his arrival in the district, was perceived as a saviour. He has classified rumours about him into three categories, according to their theme: (1) Gandhi is more powerful than all local authorities; (2) Gandhi will abolish all the obligations that peasants want to be freed of; (3) the administration of Champaran will be transferred into Indian hands, in the person of Gandhi himself. Pouchepadass has drawn attention to a process of deification of Gandhi by the local peasantry, but has stressed the fact that his image remained controlled by local dominant groups.

Shahid Amin has made a more general attempt at understanding peasant perceptions of Gandhi on the basis of the study of some writings produced in Gorakhpur district after a visit there by the Mahatma in February 1921.[24] His aim has been to reconstruct a purely 'subaltern' view of Gandhi and his message by excluding all that pertained to the influence of local dominant groups and nationalist leaders.

---

[22] B.R. Ambedkar, *What Gandhi and Congress Have Done to the Untouchables*, Bombay, Thacker, 1945.

[23] J. Pouchepadass, *Champaran and Gandhi*, Delhi, 1998.

[24] S. Amin, 'Gandhi as Mahatma: Gorakhpur District, Eastern UP, 1921–22', in R. Guha (ed.), *Subaltern Studies III: Writings on South Asian Society and History*, Delhi, 1984, pp. 1–61.

Although this may appear a slightly artificial exercise, it has the merit of bringing a degree of coherence into a corpus which would appear at first inconsistent and even extravagant. Anecdotes about Gandhi which circulated in the district and were reproduced in the local press generally credited him with supernatural powers, in particular of a thaumaturgic nature, powers which ensured that those who followed him saw their aspirations fulfilled while opponents came to grief. The dominant interpretation of the Gandhian message among the peasantry was that of incitement to social reform through purification; it strengthened the arguments of those who advocated the renunciation of alcohol and tobacco, two major preoccupations among all social reformers since the end of the nineteenth century, this being an index of 'sanskritization' as understood by M.N. Srinivas. On the other hand, non-violence as a theme appears to have had a limited impact; often, in the anecdotes circulated, those who opposed the Mahatma were violently punished for their scepticism regarding his powers, while those who followed him benefited and defeated their enemies. While Gandhi tended to preach respect for existing social hierarchies, his message was often interpreted as a call to subvert the existing order of things. These 'deviant' interpretations of the Gandhian message were often criticized by 'enlightened' elements who deplored popular superstition, but could find some nourishment in the ambiguities of Gandhi's message. For the Mahatma did not shrink from using a millenarian language which found a deep echo in his peasant audiences; thus, in February 1921 he assured the public that Swaraj would come by September of the same year.

Amin's article throws interesting light on popular reactions to Gandhi, in particular on the double process of deification and instrumentalization. For the Indian peasant masses Gandhi was a holy man because of his pure life, and at the same time a kind of deity endowed with supernatural powers which his followers could appropriate to defeat their enemies and oppressors. Some of his peasant admirers went so far as to see him as an avatar of Vishnu. The miracles attributed to him by popular rumour were sometimes rather similar to those which the Gospels credited Christ with, or those that Christian legend attributed to Saint Francis of Assisi. It was thus rumoured that Gandhi could transform wheat into sesame. These ideas could also be comic, being deployed to ridicule local grandees; or be sinister, being reputed to cause illness or infirmity in those who opposed the Mahatma.

This pattern of deification sometimes resulted in a real cult, especially among women: some made offerings to the Mahatma, others invoked his name to demand alms. Gandhi was sometimes turned into a specifically peasant deity, and, contrary to his teachings, violent actions were performed in his name. This aspect was particularly worrisome for him. There appears to have been, on the whole, a lot of misunderstanding between the Mahatma and the mass of the Indian people around the question of non-violence. It was not really because he preached non-violence that he got their support. It could even be said that he was venerated *in spite of* his commitment to non-violence, an idea which peasants found difficult to understand given the fact that violence was (and is) part of the daily environment of Indian peasants, whether exercised by the tax collector or the landlord's agent. Many of Gandhi's followers were convinced that his call to non-violence was of a purely tactical nature, meant to confuse the British. They could draw sustenance from some ambiguities in Gandhi's own discourse, in particular his widespread use of metaphors borrowed from the Hindu epics, which peasant audiences read as coded messages.

After Gandhi's death, there developed an official iconography in which he figures as the Father of the Nation and a martyr in the struggle against fanaticism and intolerance. This is the message carried in textbooks and repeated in speeches by politicians. The aim of this iconography is to project a simplified, bland image of an eminently complex and contradictory personality. It seeks to erase Gandhi's most eccentric aspects as also to obfuscate his basically religious worldview and to make him, paradoxically, a 'patron saint of Indian secularism'. This official image is not universally accepted. Beyond official speeches and ceremonies, to which people in India pay as little attention as elsewhere, perceptions of Gandhi in contemporary India remain marked by considerable diversity.

A visit to the Gandhi memorial, Rajghat, can help put this in perspective. This memorial has no monumental features: there is only a modest cenotaph in which burns a constantly rekindled flame. The Mahatma's ashes, in conformity with his wishes, were dispersed in the rivers of India. This is a monument without beauty where one is inclined to meditate in a calm setting. The atmosphere is not deeply religious: Western tourists mingle with a diverse Indian public drawn from across the country. The crowd does not appear particularly respectful; unlike the crowd which used to come to Lenin's tomb in Soviet times. There is neither worship nor worshipfulness here. Gandhi, though an icon, is not a state icon. Everyone can pay homage to him as they wish. Many in India continue to see his teachings as an inspiration and seek to adapt them to the present. For many others who are not Gandhians, he remains an inescapable reference point. One of India's recent software millionaires claims to be inspired by his theory of trusteeship in defining his own ethics of social responsibility.[25] Others see him as a purely historical figure with no message for present-day India. He also remains an object of popular veneration, though in discreet and unremarkable ways. Most Indians from the powerful to the humble, concur that he is the greatest of all Indians, and, in company with Tagore, one of the rare figures of world importance to have emerged from India in the twentieth century.

[25] See the interview of Azim Premji in *India Today*, March 2000.

CHAPTER 2

The Impossible Biography of Mohandas K. Gandhi

F ew lives have attracted as many biographers as Gandhi's, and they have come from several cultural and ideological horizons. While the attraction of Indian authors seems natural enough, the fascination shown by non-Indian writers is more intriguing. Professional biographers seem to have seen in the writing of a biography of Gandhi a particular challenge. The reason could lie in the contrast between the abundance of factual data and available comments alongside the persistence of an element of mystery. A lot is known about Gandhi's life: very few of his speeches or actions have not been reported and analysed in great detail, including by the Mahatma himself. And yet his deeper motivations continue to give rise to interrogations and speculations, which his biographers have failed to answer in a satisfactory manner. Although Gandhi's biographies may exceed a thousand (in English, more than five hundred have been listed), Gandhi remains an enigma. In his case, one could speak of a failure of biography as a literary genre. Not that some of these biographies are not valuable in limited ways; but none has established itself as *the* definitive or authoritative book on Gandhi.

Gandhi's Biographers

In Gandhi's lifetime a few biographies were written by friends or disciples such as Doke or Polak, by admirers like Romain Rolland, and by journalists such as Louis Fischer. In the aftermath of his death, the biographies have multiplied. They can be classified under four headings: hagiographies, documentary biographies, literary biographies, and interpretive biographies.

The first genre flourished mainly in India, comprising hundreds of books in English and the various Indian languages. Hagiography often means martyrology: these works generally present Gandhi as a martyr in the struggle for freedom and against fanaticism. They emphasize his self-sacrifice for the cause of Indian unity, beyond religious divisions, and underline his exceptional human qualities. The genre is also represented outside India, for instance in France by the works of Camille Drevet,[1] a peace activist who was the secretary of the 'groupe des amis de Gandhi' for many years and who sought to spread the Gandhian message in France. She tended to see Gandhi as a kind of Christian saint, as did many other authors in England and America.

The documentary genre has been the almost exclusive preserve of Indian authors, culminating in Tendulkar's massive eight volume-work published in the 1950s and 1960s.[2] B.R. Nanda's one-volume work[3] is probably the best documentary synthesis available and has been reprinted several times. After these two, there seems to have been place only for more limited books dealing with specific aspects of Gandhi's life. To the same documentary genre belong the monumental *Collected Works* in ninety volumes,[4] which are a mine for the researcher, in spite of certain lacunae and a critical apparatus which is often insufficient.

The last three decades have been marked by the efflorescence of literary and/or interpretive biographies. These have been generally written by authors other than professional historians, without any knowledge of the historical context. From this vast corpus of works of unequal quality, mostly written in English by Indian, British and American authors, a few stand out by the quality of the writing or the originality of the point of view. Erikson's attempt at writing a psycho-biography of the Mahatma[5] is one of the most interesting. He seeks to

---

[1] C. Drevet, *Gandhi, sa vie, son œuvre, avec un exposé de sa philosophie*, Paris, 1967.

[2] D.G. Tendulkar, *Mahatma: Life of Mohandas Karamchand Gandhi*, New Delhi, 1960–3, 8 vols.

[3] B.R. Nanda, *Mahatma Gandhi: A Biography*, Delhi, 1989 (1st edn, London, 1958).

[4] *The Collected Works of Mahatma Gandhi*, New Delhi, 1958–84, 90 vols.

[5] E.H. Erikson, *Gandhi's Truth*, New York, 1969.

interpret Gandhi's trajectory through an analysis of the traumas of his childhood, particularly his relationship to his father, using Gandhi's autobiography as his source and supplementing it with interviews of people who were close to Gandhi. In spite of pretensions to analytic detachment, Erikson cannot help condemning Gandhi for his failures as a father, which he relates to the Mahatma's pathological relationship to his own father. He ends his analysis (in both senses of the term) with a close reading of an episode in Gandhi's career—his intervention in a workers' strike in Ahmedabad in 1918, which he sees as particularly significant. He draws attention to the existence of a deep inner conflict within Gandhi between 'phallism' and saintliness, between paternal potency and maternal solicitude. This could be seen in clinical terms as Gandhi's neurosis, but according to Erikson it is also the bedrock of his self-construction as an individual. He sees in Gandhi's 'maternal' side (noted by many) a reflection of a primitive matriarchal religion impregnating popular Hinduism. He reads this as a somewhat prophetic prediction of the devaluation of the martial model of masculinity, and as opening the way to a freer and mutual identification between the genders. He finds the source of non-violence within this inner conflict of Gandhi's personality. His book distinguishes itself from the run-of-the mill by its sharp intelligence, but its intuitions have remained unverified and it seems something of a failed attempt.

The celebration of Gandhi's centenary in 1969 led to a spate of biographies of a more literary bent. Those written by Geoffrey Ashe[6] and Robert Payne[7] stand out as particularly representative of the trend which arose in the late 1960s. The new conventional wisdom on Gandhi departed from the older one inasmuch as it eschewed attempts to make Gandhi a Christian saint and tried to take more into account the Indian cultural context—although the relationship of Gandhi to Hinduism remained a difficult problem for these authors. The emerging vision of Gandhi was that of a secular politician whose methods of political struggle and type of leadership were of greater interest than his views on religion. Geoffrey Ashe's book, subtitled 'A Study in Revolution', was the closest attempt to a political biography of

[6] G. Ashe, *Gandhi: A Study in Revolution*, op. cit., 1968.
[7] R. Payne, *The Life and Death of Mahatma Gandhi*, New York, 1969.

Gandhi, while Payne's covered a wider range of issues. There was a return to the perception of Gandhi as a revolutionary, which echoed the 1920s and 1930s, and was certainly a direct reflection of the political atmosphere of the 1960s. The cyclical return of certain kinds of representation is a law for the biographical genre, especially when it is practised over a long period of time in relation to the same subject. Actually, in almost every decade Gandhi has been reinvented, and this has been done by drawing on the extraordinary 'polysemy' of a multifaceted figure. In spite of these two biographers' efforts at objectivity, they could not escape the fascination of their subject and tended to depict Gandhi as a hero of the century, with his struggle being a kind of modern epic.

The Gandhian renewal of the 1970s and 1980s brought in its wake a host of books on various aspects of life, thought and action, but few general biographies. The late 1980s saw a new kind of Gandhi biography, which seemed to reflect a deepening of empirical knowledge—made possible by the completion of the *Collected Works*—and at the same time the emergence of a more distanced approach, probably due to the passage of time. Two of these biographies seem to embody some of the new features, but they also reveal the growing fragmentation and increasing richness of Gandhian studies. Judith Brown's biography[8] is a synthesis of the more advanced historical research, and one of its great merits is to give proper attention to the last years of Gandhi's life, which tended to be neglected by biographers. Brown emphasizes the tragic side of Gandhi's final years, when this 'prisoner of hope' had to witness the violence of partition, the negation of his lifework. This does not lead Brown to proclaim Gandhi a failure: for her the Mahatma was a man confronted with a historical situation in which he had been an important actor but which he did not master. What comes out of this study is Gandhi's humanity rather than his saintliness. Although historically accurate and finely tuned, this work fails somewhat to unearth the overall complexity of Gandhi. The same is true of Martin Green's more limited exercise,[9] geared towards elucidating Gandhi's complex relationship to 'New Age' thought as it flourished in the late Victorian era, including such radical critiques of the Indus-

[8] J.M. Brown, *Gandhi: Prisoner of Hope*, New Haven and London, 1989.
[9] M. Green, *Gandhi: Voice of a New Age Revolution*, New York, 1993.

trial Revolution as Edward Carpenter and Leo Tolstoi. Green shows convincingly how much Gandhi's adhesion to that ideology had an impact on his thought, leading to that idiosyncratic mixture of modernism and traditionalism which so astonished his contemporaries. Green is also critical of Erikson's strictures against Gandhi's role as a father and puts forward an alternative analysis of his psyche. Biographers now seem to have become more alert to Gandhi's complex personality, and view his achievements in a more realistic light.

On the whole, the existing corpus of Gandhi biographies cannot but provoke a feeling of frustration. Apart from the small number of books that seem worth mentioning there is a mass of work which seldom displays real originality in approach: most biographies are content to rehash, *ad nauseam*, with more or less detail thrown in, the same episodes drawn from Gandhi's autobiography. The most interesting, either because of their literary qualities or the depth of their interpretations, distance themselves from the hagiographical mode which has long dominated the field. But even the better works do not give satisfactory answers to all the important questions surrounding this most complex and contradictory individual. It seems fair to say that we are not likely to be get a really satisfactory or definitive biography of Gandhi. We should try to understand why.

Gandhi and the Limitations of Biography
as a Genre

One of the major difficulties for biographers is Gandhi's late entry into 'high history'—when he was around fifty—an entry which nothing in his early life allowed anyone to foresee. In this sense, his trajectory differs from other political figures of the twentieth century. The three periods into which his life can be clearly divided—namely childhood and youth culminating in the departure to South Africa in 1893; the South African years between 1893 and 1915; and the Indian period of 1915–47, stand out as three separate lives. The thread running through them is not easily discernible. Gandhi himself, in the preface to his *Autobiography,* implicitly refuted the view that his biography could be written as one story. He perceived his life as a succession of 'experiments with truth' rather than as a continuum. If most existing biographies give the impression of an assemblage of some-what disjointed fragments, it is neither for lack of documentation nor understanding on the part of the biographers; it is rather a reflection of the man's discontinuous life. Perhaps Gandhi's case is simply a paradigm: all human lives are marked by discontinuities and the appa-rent coherence of biographical narrative is largely an artefact of dis-course. With Gandhi, biography is, as a genre, subjected to the most severe of tests, for the continuity between the child and youth on the one hand and the mature adult on the other is particularly difficult to establish. The young Gandhi did not display features of a strong per-sonality and seemed ill-adapted to social life, while the mature Gandhi developed an unusually strong and even eccentric personality.

So Gandhi's childhood and youth remain relatively obscure parts of his life. In his autobiographical narrative Gandhi devoted only a few pages to them, focusing largely on his early marriage, which he saw as a terrible blemish, and overlooking many aspects which could have been clues to his personality. Pyarelal's book[10] provides some extra in-formation, thanks to testimonies from family members, but on the whole that period remains shrouded in mystery. Most biographies give it short shrift (Judith Brown gives it twenty pages in a 400-page book). The difficulty felt by biographers is largely of a historiographical nature. Modern Indian history has focused mostly on the study of those parts of India which were under direct colonial rule, while the hundreds of indirectly ruled princely states have been relatively neg-lected. This makes it difficult to reconstruct the socio-political context in which the Mahatma spent his childhood and part of his youth. A lot of attention has been paid to the immediate family environment, particularly to Gandhi's parents, at the expense of a broader contextual study, which would necessitate a proper micro-historical approach.

As for Gandhi himself, he dwelt at considerable length on his Eng-lish stay, which is therefore always given pride of place in biographies. But in his account of it he gave disproportionate importance to a few anecdotes, to the detriment of detailed information on his intellectual and professional development. As a result, biographers have not de-voted much attention to his very specific relationship with the law, nor

[10] Pyarelal, *Mahatma Gandhi: The Early Phase*, Ahmedabad, 1965.

tried to explain his paradoxical combination of scrupulous respect for the law alongside bold opposition to laws he deemed unfair—a striking feature of his whole career.

However, the real black hole in Gandhi's life is his stay in South Africa, despite the fact that it is well documented. Gandhi himself wrote two different accounts of this period: a fairly factual one in *Satyagraha in South Africa*,[11] and a more personal interpretation in the 200-page section of the *Autobiography*[12] which is devoted to the South African years. Both those narratives were written in the 1920s, more than ten years after Gandhi's departure from South Africa, entirely from memory, without the help of written notes, and serious doubts exist as to the reliability of such personal memories uncorroborated by other testimonies. Particularly problematic is the lack of independent sources from Indians in South Africa. The evidence available consists mainly on the one hand of a massive array of official sources from both the South African and British authorities, which are mostly useful to confirm or invalidate specific statements, and on the other hand of newspapers and some narratives by Gandhi's European friends such as Henry Polak and his wife. Next to nothing is known of the way in which Gandhi was perceived by the Muslim merchants with whom he was closely associated, for they have apparently left few written traces. Most biographers, with two exceptions, have therefore tended to closely follow Gandhi's own narrative without questioning the authenticity of his claims.

As a result, a crucial period of Gandhi's life, during which the timid young lawyer who landed in Durban at the age of twenty-four turned into a mature forty-five-year-old activist in full intellectual bloom, has remained largely outside the scope of the careful scrutiny applied to Gandhi's later life in India. During that twenty-one-year period, Gandhi took at least two decisions which decisively affected the shape of his life, namely the decision to devote himself to a full-time public career, and the decision to cease sexual relations with his wife and

[11] M.K. Gandhi, *Satyagraha in South Africa*, Ahmedabad, 1928 (translated by Valji Desai from the Gujarati edition published in 1924).

[12] M.K. Gandhi, *An Autobiography: The Story of My Experiments with Truth*, London, 1972, translated from the Gujarati by Mahadev Desai (1st edn, Ahmedabad, 1927).

abandon family life for community life. The importance of this period for a proper understanding of Gandhi's personality cannot be over-emphasized, yet despite Gandhi's own narratives and the attempts of some biographers to enlarge the scope of their enquiry, the inner motivations for these crucial decisions largely elude us.

The major problem would appear to be that of contextualization. South African colonial society, such as it existed in the late-nineteenth and early-twentieth century, is such a remote universe for the mostly Indian, British and American biographers of the Mahatma, that an enormous effort of imagination is necessary to reconstruct the environment in which Gandhi was led to these momentous choices. It is therefore easier for most biographers to accept Gandhi's own summary explanations. His narrative puts the major emphasis on the dilemmas of an individual conscience confronted with the evidence of oppression. Gandhi tried to show how, through a process of purification of which the catalyst was a deep spiritual crisis, he chanced upon the notion of disinterested service to the community.

One could well ask why a spiritual crisis should result in choosing public action in favour of a relatively privileged merchant group. For it must be borne in mind that, prior to 1906–7, Gandhi's activity remained largely confined to the tiny milieu of mostly Muslim Gujarati merchants who formed the bulk of the élite within the Indian community in South Africa. Only in 1913–14—when he included among the objectives of his last satyagraha campaign the abolition of the three-pound tax that indentured labourers had to pay to stay in South Africa at the expiry of their indenture contract—did Gandhi's action really address the problems of the indentured workers, who accounted for the vast majority of South African Indians, particularly those in Natal. Gandhi's motivations during the first fifteen years of his South African stay were complex and likely to have undergone a change over time. To my knowledge, only two authors have been bold enough to raise this type of interrogation: T.K. Mahadevan, the iconoclastic 'Gandhian' in his book on the beginnings of Gandhi's South African stay,[13] and the South African historian Maureen Swan in her excellent book on Gandhi and South African Indians.[14] The latter's

[13] T.K. Mahadevan, *The Year of the Phoenix*, Delhi, 1982.
[14] M. Swan, *Gandhi: The South African Experience*, Johannesburg, 1985.

merit in particular is to recover the agency of South African Indians in the making of their own history. Most biographers have tended to write a purely 'Gandhi-centred' account of the Mahatma's South African years, in which his fellow countrymen figure only as background or, at best, as admirers applauding the future great man. A good instance of this perspective is provided by Geoffrey Ashe's otherwise interesting book: 'The drama has only one fully realized character, under a constant spotlight. Gandhi is the master spirit, while most of his companions, with all their zeal and goodwill, are simply names. . . .'[15] The same author, nevertheless, is led to remark that anyone who has met Indian merchants finds it improbable that they were in reality as shadowy as they appear in most narratives. Their shadowy nature is wrongly and simplistically assumed from the fact that they did not leave written testimonies. As for Gandhi, he was engaged in an introspective exercise in which there was only limited space for other people (although in his *Satyagraha in South Africa* he gives some importance to one of his fellow activists, a Muslim merchant named Seth Kachhalia). It is more than likely that Gandhi was moulded by South African Indian society—possibly more than he moulded it. A model of reciprocal interaction between the activist and the society in which he operated appears more plausible than the existing one-sided models.

Maureen Swan's book, unfortunately little noticed when it was published, allows us to better appraise some aspects of this interaction. We are informed that the Indian merchants of Natal had not waited for Gandhi's arrival to create an embryo organization, the Durban Indian Committee, and to start, as early as January 1891, a campaign in defence of their interests and against the granting of self-government to white settlers (which, they rightly predicted, would result in increased discrimination against them). After self-government was granted to Natal in 1893, they sought to develop a more permanent activity for which they needed a full-time organizer. Gandhi, with his knowledge of English and Gujarati and his familiarity with the British legal system, was perfectly suited to the task. Between 1894 and 1906, he was the chosen representative of the Indian commercial community in its struggle to attenuate the discriminatory measures taken by the

---

[15] G. Ashe, *Gandhi*, op. cit., p.67.

colonial authorities in Natal and Transvaal, and there is nothing in his public activities which suggests anything beyond that. His transformation from simple spokesman into leader was a fairly sudden process which started in 1906–7, in which the response of the community was at least as important as Gandhi's own initiatives. There was a dialectical relationship between the growing mobilization of the Indian community in Transvaal—which tended to transcend the boundaries of the merchant élite to encompass a larger group of itinerant pedlars—and the evolution of Gandhi's political ideas.

Gandhi, whose personal philosophy had taken shape in the first years of the twentieth century under the double influence of Ruskin and Tolstoi, saw the possibility of translating his ideas into political practice; he found it increasingly necessary, in order to overcome the limitations which were inherent in the merchant milieu—such as its atomization and general apathy—to create a hard core of activists with a belief in the importance of morality for political action. During the first satyagraha campaign, from 1908, Gandhi succeeded in making his moral leadership the driving engine of the movement. This allowed him to enlarge his appeal beyond a purely merchant base. In the course of this movement, Gandhi was able to formulate, with increasing clarity, the principles of his action within the framework of the ideology of satyagraha. The transformation occurred as a result of his dialectical relationship to the Indian milieu in Transvaal and cannot be accounted for in purely spiritual terms, even if most of his readers, including the majority of his biographers, appear to be convinced by his own explanations.

Thanks to the discovery of the method of satyagraha, Gandhi was also able to envisage going back to India and taking part in the political struggle there. A decisive step in the process of Gandhi's political maturation took place in 1913, when faced with a wilting movement and the growing opposition from the élite in Natal. Gandhi responded now by enlarging the appeal of the struggle to include specific groups of indentured workers, such as the coal-miners of Newcastle, among whom he found at last the determined hard core he needed to pursue the struggle. The call on workers was partly a response to Gandhi's growing difficulty in his attempt at mobilizing merchants, who tended to look for a compromise. Swan's excellent work helps us understand the contribution of the social milieu of South African Indians to the transformations in Gandhi's vision and political action.

Gandhi's future biographers will have to take better account of this growing body of literature on the Indian community in South Africa. Here the young lawyer, pathologically shy, grew into a public figure capable of addressing and leading crowds. It is clear that there remain vast obscure areas in the Mahatma's life. The process by which a small-time lawyer became a mahatma remains mysterious. Part of the mystery is caused by Gandhi himself: his *Autobiography* tries to cover his tracks so as to discourage all attempts at reading his trajectory in worldly terms. The Gandhian myth originates in Gandhi.

Gandhi as His Own Biographer:
The *Autobiography*

After having read the French writer's essay on him, Gandhi wrote to Romain Rolland on 22 March 1924: 'It matters little that you made a few mistakes in your Essai. The wonder, for me, is that you made so few and that, in spite of living in a different and remote atmosphere, you succeeded in interpreting so truthfully my message.' Although he gratefully acknowledges the homage paid him by one of the West's most prestigious intellectuals, Gandhi soon shows a desire to keep control of his own legend. He says, half-jokingly, that he wrote the *Autobiography* largely to correct the errors in Rolland's book. In fact he started writing it while in jail, at the behest of two co-workers. It was first published serially in the form of articles in his paper *Navajivan*, and was translated from Gujarati into English by his secretary Mahadev Desai, being published as a book for the first time in 1927. This extraordinary piece of writing is certainly much more than a response to Romain Rolland. Gandhi declared he was not trying to write an autobiography, which he felt was a purely Western genre, but simply narrating a series of 'experiments with truth' through which his character and personality had been shaped. In his Introduction he underlines the fact that his experiments in the *political* field were widely known, even beyond India, and were for him, in any case, of limited value: 'But I should certainly like to narrate my experiments in the spiritual field which are known only to myself, and from which

I have derived such power as I possess for working in the political field.'[16]

Written from memory, without the help of notes, the text presents itself as a succession of reflections and anecdotes that are intended to retrace a spiritual itinerary, not to narrate a life in all its worldly aspects. It is not a linear narration and there are numerous digressions which seek very deliberately to break the continuity of the account. Gandhi's aim is to make his reader ponder at each stage the deeper meaning of the episode narrated, to prevent him giving himself up to the flow of words. This structure allows Gandhi to select just those episodes he deems significant.

In spite of his warnings to the contrary, Gandhi managed to establish his text as the main factual source for all his later biographies, at least for the period of his life before 1920 (the year in which the autobiography ends). Astonishingly even Gandhi's most improbable statements have been accepted uncritically by most of his biographers. Let us focus on one of the key events in his life—his decision, taken in 1894, to remain in South Africa after the expiration of his contract with his first employer. His first biographers, and Romain Rolland after them, interpreted the episode in a simple and unconvincing manner. Rolland wrote:

> When the time came, he was in a hurry to go back, when he was informed that the government was preparing a bill which deprived Indians of their last franchises. The South African Indians were without strength to struggle, without will, unorganized, demoralized. They needed a leader, a soul. Gandhi sacrificed himself. He stayed.[17]

In his own account written from memory more than thirty years after the facts, Gandhi had given an extraordinarily detailed account of the episode,[18] which should at least have raised some doubts as to its reliability. His version was that, having gone to a farewell reception given in his honour by his employer, he chanced upon a newspaper article about a bill presented before the Legislative Assembly of Natal which proposed to deprive 'free' Indians of the right to vote. His

[16] Gandhi, *Autobiography*, op. cit., p.12.
[17] R. Rolland, *Mahatma Gandhi*, op. cit., p. 18.
[18] Gandhi, *Autobiography*, op. cit., pp. 115–17.

curiosity alerted, Gandhi asked some Indian merchants about it: they appeared unaware of the bill and its possible implications. Gandhi then explained to them that it was only the beginning of a process which would gather momentum and eventually lead to an unbearable situation for Indians in Natal. The merchants thereupon spontaneously asked him to stay on and help them fight the bill, promising to pay him for his services. Gandhi saw in this episode a clear manifestation of divine providence: 'Thus God laid the foundations of my life in South Africa and sowed the seed of the fight for national self-respect.'[19]

This account, as T.K. Mahadevan says in his iconoclastic text,[20] is full of inconsistencies. It is highly unlikely that rich Gujarati merchants in Durban were unaware of the existence of a bill which so directly concerned them. It also seems extremely unlikely that they suddenly decided, without prior confabulation, to employ Gandhi. Yet this fairly implausible version of the episode is to be found in practically all of Gandhi's biographies. Robert Payne, a scrupulous biographer, reproduces it *in extenso* in his 1969 book, and twenty years later Judith Brown gives a summary version. With Gandhi as the sole source of the episode, prudence might at least have led biographers to suspend judgement.

I have dwelt at length on this not in order to blame authors or defend a positivist conception of history, but to show the extraordinary authority attributed to Gandhi as the principal and often only factual source of his own life, in spite of his own denials regarding the nature of his project. Why do experienced biographers and historians abandon all critical sense when it comes to Gandhi? The answer lies at least partly in the magic of Gandhi's writing, which casts a spell few can resist. Gandhi's narration, even in Mahadev Desai's translation (which, according to specialists, leaves much to be desired, despite having been partly revised by Gandhi himself), is as limpid and as free-flowing as some passages of the New Testament, so much so that one hesitates to break its continuity by raising questions of historical criticism: those appear so out of place.

Gandhi's writing strategy is not always easy to comprehend, but it is extraordinarily effective. His writing is simple, verging on an auster-

[19] Ibid., p. 117.
[20] Mahadevan, *The Year of the Phoenix*, op. cit.

ity which yet does not prevent the text from being pleasant and full of such conviction as to ensnare even the most hardened sceptic. Gandhi manages to address both an Indian public and a Western public, his prose possessing a double register of familiarity and strangeness. Close reading of the text also reveals a clear desire in Gandhi to keep clear of Christian interpetations of his life and give central place to Hindu spirituality for his processes of identity formation. His inclusion, among his spiritual masters, of the little-known Gujarati poet Raychand-bhai Mehta, who is put on the same footing as Ruskin and Tolstoi—names familiar to his Western audience—is typical of his intention. Gandhi often felt a kind of vicarious pleasure in surprising readers with his many idiosyncrasies. Although he is rather vague about the exact nature of his spiritual relationship to Raychandbhai, he accords him central place in the account of his religious evolution. While some of his Christian friends attempted to convert him, a letter from Ray-chandbhai helped in rekindling his shaken belief in Hinduism, and inciting him to study Hindu texts further.

The trajectory Gandhi wants to outline is a slow ascent towards enlightenment. He pictures himself as an ordinary adolescent, remote from God, sometimes succumbing to the temptations of the world but endowed with an acute sense of the difference between good and evil. In London he was exposed to the moral perils of a great metropolis but was able to escape them and, through vegetarianism and the discovery of Hindu sacred texts, began re-sourcing himself in his own tradition. Despite having rejected atheism he was still far from God. During his South African years he was gradually able, through meditation and action, to transform himself into a less imperfect being, sensitive to the idea and presence of the divine. In this narrative, public action appears only in passing. There is thus no explanation of the change in his political ideas, nor of his gradual loss of faith in the benevolence of British rule. His actions are presented as responses to an internal necessity of a spiritual nature. The morality of political action is not defined in relation to abstract principles but only to its conformity with the dictum of conscience. He expresses no regret for his support to the British at the time of the Boer War or of the First World War, since they answered the dictum of his conscience at those times.

There is a striking contrast between Gandhi's own strictures on his

private behaviour and his total lack of self-doubt regarding his public
actions. While he does not hesitate to lambast, in the harshest terms,
his behaviour towards his wife or his children, his public life escapes
criticism and he invariably presents himself as having the purest intentions. This dichotomy appears puzzling in view of the fact that he
always refused any separation between the private and public spheres,
conceiving of any human grouping as a more or less enlarged form of
the family. Gandhi put forward the idea that, if he succeeded in be-
having in an exemplary manner in his private life (and here the crucial
point is the strict observance of brahmacharya), his public actions
would be exemplary too. The problem he faced was finding ways of
applying his personal morality to the realm of political action. For him
this was a technical rather than a metaphysical question, to which he
thought he had found the appropriate answer in the form of satyagraha.
He had no notion of progress in the political sphere; the only possible
progress was spiritual: the more strictly he observed his vows of celibacy, the better the *satyagrahi* he would be. Yet while he was ready to
acknowledge sexual lapses, he was little inclined to political self-criti-
cism except to explain some of his failures as stemming from insufficient
purity.

One can't help feeling that Gandhi was also trying to cover his
tracks. He is keen to refute the widespread view of him as a Christian
saint, giving great importance to episodes which show him in a poor
light—one cannot exclude the hypothesis of strong masochistic ten-
dencies—and presenting his religious trajectory as particularly chaotic.
While recognizing the influence of his Christian friends, he took great
care to reaffirm his attachment to Hindu texts. He even recounted an
episode in which he compared Buddha and Christ, to the advantage
of the former, because his love went out to all creatures, while Christ's
was directed mostly to humans. This choice was not haphazard and
reveals his desire to distance himself from the Christian image of him
projected by his Western admirers. His way of presenting his religious
views was to show them as developing into an original synthesis out of
a Hindu hard core, but he was never much interested in doctrinal
exactitude. At the same time, the picture he drew of himself and his
insistence on putting forward his moral scruples at each juncture was
not exactly meant to deter the Western reader from the idea of his

saintliness. Towards his Indian readers, some of whom went as far as seeing him as a deity, his strategy was, on the one hand, to display all his imperfections, and on the other to distance himself from traditional Hinduism, especially on the question of untouchability and relations with Muslims. He was well aware that the account of his spiritual itinerary could only reinforce perceptions of his saintliness but did nothing to prevent this.

By writing the *Autobiography*, Gandhi sought to take charge of all subsequent representations of his own life, and to impose an interpretation in terms of his spiritual quest which ought not to be seriously questioned afterwards. This was not a deliberate attempt by Gandhi to mislead the public. On the contrary, by insisting that he did not write an account of his life, but only of his spiritual itinerary, Gandhi pre-empted criticism directed at factual aspects of his narrative. There remains the lingering feeling that this caveat was of a mostly rhetorical nature. For in 1927 Gandhi was no more the obscure leader of a group of Indian coolies in South Africa; he was Mahatma Gandhi, the recognized leader of the struggle of three hundred million Indians against British imperialism, and this gave his writings a particular aura of authority. Who, after such a book had been published—apart from open political adversaries—would dare propose another interpretation of Gandhi's life ? Even Erikson's attempt at deconstructing Gandhi's life by using psychoanalysis came up against the fact that his materials were basically derived from the *Autobiography*. To systematically deconstruct Gandhi's life, what is needed at first is a systematic deconstruction of that Ur-text, the *Autobiography*. Short of that difficult task, there remain his writings and his public actions, which are rich material.

CHAPTER 3

Gandhi's Posthumous Life

I n the course of the five decades following Gandhi's death, the image posterity has formed of him underwent constant change. In India his memory became the site of an ongoing political debate. Outside India he has been mostly credited with the invention of a method of political struggle deemed of universal value, namely non-violence. He has also been viewed as the founder of a doctrine, Gandhism, which at one time appeared to offer a kind of third way between capitalism and communism. With the end of the Cold War and the advent of globalization, the dominant representation of Gandhi in India as well as the world at large has become that of a forerunner of ecology and alternative movements.

Gandhi in India
After 1948: A Disputed Legacy

In the wake of Gandhi's assassination his memory was immediately appropriated for the purposes of ongoing political struggles. The outpouring of popular grief was channelized by Nehru in a well-defined direction. As the Indian Prime Minister, who had enjoyed a close personal relationship with the Mahatma, Nehru was seen as his natural political heir. In a series of interventions he used Gandhi's martyrdom as a weapon to fight against those within the Congress and elsewhere who tried to steer India away from the 'secular' course defined during the freedom struggle, and against advocates of a policy of discrimination in relation to India's Muslims. The subcontinent was just emerging from a frenzy of killing in Punjab and some were tempted by the idea of a mass expulsion of Muslims. Nehru defined his line in a speech at the ceremony for the immersion of Gandhi's ashes. In a previous speech he had declared the assassin a mad man; on this occasion he put forward a different interpretation:

Our country gave birth to a mighty soul and he shone like a beacon not only for India but for the whole world. And yet he was done to death by one of our own brothers and compatriots. How did this happen? You might think that it was an act of madness, but that does not explain this tragedy. It could only occur because the seed for it was sown in the poison of hatred and enmity that spread throughout the country and affected so many of our people. Out of that seed grew this poisonous plant. It is the duty of all of us to fight the poison of hatred and ill-will. If we have learnt anything from Gandhiji, we must bear no ill-will or enmity towards any person. The individual is not our enemy. It is the poison within him that we fight and which we must put an end to. . . .'[1]

For those who listened to Nehru there was no doubt as to the identity of the poison, that is, the Hindu extremism preached by the RSS and the Hindu Mahasabha. Although no proof of direct RSS responsibility in the plot was presented, that organization became the target of popular demonstrations which sometimes erupted into violence and, after a while, the RSS was officially banned.

Nathuram Godse, Gandhi's assassin and main defendant in the Gandhi murder trial which opened in May 1948 in Delhi's Red Fort (traditionally the scene of India's great political trials), tried to use the courtroom as a political forum by reading a long declaration in which he attempted to justify his crime. He accused Gandhi of complacence towards Muslims, blamed him for the sufferings of Partition, and generally criticized his subjectivism and pretension to a monopoly of the truth. Although his attacks met with some echo in high-caste Hindu circles traditionally hostile to Gandhi, he could not create a groundswell of opinion in his favour. Godse's declarations and motivations have been appraised in the most contradictory fashion. While Robert Payne, in his detailed account of the trial, dwells on the irrational nature of his statement,[2] Ashis Nandy underlines the deeply rational character of Godse's action, which, in his view, reflected well-founded fears among upper-caste Hindus of Gandhi's message and its impact on Hindu society.[3] The trial was quickly expedited, and Godse

[1] 'Speech of 12 February 1948', *Jawaharlal Nehru's Speeches*, vol. I, September 1946–May 1949, New Delhi, 1949, p. 49.

[2] R. Payne, *The Life and Death of Mahatma Gandhi*, op. cit., p. 641.

[3] A. Nandy, 'Final Encounter: The Politics of the Assassination of Gandhi', *At the Edge of Psychology: Essays in Politics and Culture*, Delhi, 1980, p. 87.

and his accomplice Apte executed in November 1949 after the rejection of their last appeal (in spite of Gandhi's son's intervention pleading mercy). The haste with which they were tried, indicted and executed is sometimes attributed to Home Minister Vallabhbhai Patel's desire to avoid scrutiny of the failure to prevent the assassination.

Popular anger at the murder was rekindled by the trial and helped Nehru successfully confront the rise of extremist ideas within the Hindu community as well as isolate the upholders of discrimination against Muslims and confrontation with Pakistan. The revelation of a certain amount of negligence in surveillance and protection around Gandhi gave him the edge in his struggle with Patel over the control of Congress (the latter's death in 1950 left him in sole command).

Largely thanks to the revulsion felt by many towards Gandhi's assassins, a consensus was re-established around the secular values which had been under threat from Hindu extremists capitalizing on the massacres of Partition, and the Hindu Right found itself excluded from any significant role in political life (it re-emerged only after 1977). Gandhi's death was thus made instrumental by his political heirs, in particular Nehru, to draw a clear line between secular nationalists and anti-secularists who, tarnished by their association with Gandhi's assassination, were considered 'anti-national' and beyond the pale. Making Gandhi the 'Father of the Nation' and constructing an official memory around him were meant not only as homage but answered immediate political exigencies. The question that arose was whether, in response to Pakistan—which tried to present itself as the state for the Muslims of the subcontinent—India was to identify itself as the state of the Hindus. This was the position advocated by Hindu extremists and those in the Congress close to them; the alternative chosen was that it should remain faithful to the secular ideals which had been those of Congress during the freedom struggle.

Gandhi's official image was carefully constructed so as to make him the founding father of secular nationalism, which Nehru sought to promote as the ideology of the new republic. For Nehru, the stakes were also very personal. In relation to Gandhi he was led to ponder over the question of the difficult balance between strong leadership and democracy. In his 1951 preface to the first edition of Tendulkar's official biography of Gandhi,[4] he mused over the dilemma of the political leader tempted towards compromise to court popular approval, and thus in danger of losing sight of ideals. He recalled with longing Gandhi's ability to remain fixed to his ideals while keeping contact with the masses, a feat Nehru himself found increasingly difficult to emulate. The image of Gandhi, who was like a father to him, weighed heavily on Nehru's shoulders, reminding him constantly of his own growing isolation *vis-à-vis* his people, of the gradual dissolution of the ideal he had fought for. For Nehru, turning the Mahatma into an icon served the double purpose of answering direct political needs and alleviating the burden of his conscience.

For several years after his death, Gandhi's shadow loomed large over the political life of the new Indian Republic. Nehru, after isolating and quelling the Hindu Right and its Congress accomplices, was then confronted with a new challenge, also thrown at him in the name of Gandhi. Some of the Mahatma's closest disciples were disappointed with the economic and social policies followed by independent India, which they thought contrary to Gandhi's ideas. Without frontally opposing Congress, they formed various organizations which sought to advance a specifically Gandhian agenda of social and economic reform; Gandhi had always been active in such kinds of social organizations. Unhappy with the official image of a 'Father of the Nation' whose social and economic ideals the nation did not espouse, they sought to project an alternative image of Gandhi as a social reformer and drew attention to the enormous gap between Gandhian ideals and Indian social reality.

Two different trends emerged among those 'Gandhians' who challenged the policies of India's new leaders. One group of disciples, led by Vinoba Bhave, who had been the closest to Gandhi towards the end of his life, chose a resolutely non-political path and gave precedence to social reform, focusing on the agrarian question, one of the most pressing issues confronting India. In 1951 Vinoba Bhave launched the Bhoodan movement, aimed at obtaining (through persuasion) a

---

[4] 'Preface', in D.G. Tendulkar, *Mahatma*, op. cit., vol. 1, New Delhi, 1951 (1st edn).

massive redistribution of land in favour of the poorest. The movement started in Telengana in the former princely state of Hyderabad, where a particularly unequal distribution of land had favoured the emergence of peasant guerrillas led by the Communists. With some support from the government, Vinoba Bhave toured the Indian countryside, attempting to persuade landlords to donate land to the landless. He was successful on paper, as millions of acres were thus donated. These consisted, however, almost exclusively of infertile or marginal lands, and the donations had no significant impact on the agrarian problem. Vinoba Bhave tended to present his movement as a direct continuation of Gandhi's work. Gandhi had struggled for swaraj, which had been obtained; it was necessary to get to the next stage, the fight for *sarvodaya* (welfare for all). Other methods were needed at that stage: the target was not now an alien imperial power but compatriots who had to be persuaded, not coerced. Satyagraha as a method of struggle was no more appropriate, precisely because of the element of coercion involved in it.

Many of Gandhi's disciples rallied to Vinoba Bhave's call, but a minority followed another presumptive heir, the socialist leader Rammanohar Lohia, who advocated mass struggle to achieve social change.[5] Lohia came from a background different from Vinoba's: he had belonged to the Congress Socialist Left, influenced by Marxism. An incisive polemicist and influential ideologue, he attempted a synthesis between Gandhism and socialism. In 1954 he called on the Socialists to renounce violent struggle and adopt Gandhian methods of mass action. After he had become secretary of the Socialist Party in 1955, he organized a series of satyagrahas aimed at removing English as the official language, fighting casteism, fixing the prices of essential commodities, and saving the Himalayan forests. He opted for a policy of confrontation with Nehru, and the latter, who had some ideological affinities with Lohia, was led to edge closer to Vinoba Bhave, in order to isolate Lohia, whom he saw as a trouble-maker. In spite of his undoubted charisma, Lohia found himself increasingly alone and did not succeed in making any lasting impact on Indian politics. By the early 1960s his failure was obvious.

[5] On Bhave and Lohia, see in particular R.G. Fox, *Gandhian Utopia: Experiments with Culture*, Boston, 1989, pp. 173–6.

Thus, in the aftermath of Gandhi's death, his legacy in India was claimed by Nehru, Vinoba Bhave and Lohia. Nehru's claim to it was the most general; he presented Gandhi as the overall inspiration of Indian nationalism and model leader, but he did not seek to follow specific Gandhian policies since he considered many of Gandhi's social and economic ideas as either obsolete or utopian. He encouraged Vinoba Bhave's apolitical movement to give an outlet to some of Gandhi's faithful disciples, and also in the hope that it would help defuse social tensions in the countryside. For his part, Vinoba Bhave presented himself as Gandhi's heir in his role as a social reformer, eschewing confrontation with Nehru and his government. Lohia tried to appear as Gandhi's radical heir and sought to create a properly Indian form of socialism which he saw as an alternative both to Nehru's Westernized model of socialism and to Vinoba's apoliticism.

It was left to another politician, Jayaprakash Narayan (JP), to capture Gandhi's mantle and use it effectively in the political struggle. JP was an ex-Congress Socialist who had been instrumental in the creation of the Socialist Party in 1948. In the 1950s, disillusioned with Marxism, he converted to Gandhism and became a key organizer in Vinoba's movement. While the latter continued to pin his hopes on the Bhoodan movement, in the early 1970s JP decided the moment had come to rejoin political struggle and he launched a Gandhian-style struggle for a 'Total Revolution' in Bihar which set him on a collision course with Indira Gandhi. His arrest in 1975 during the Emergency gave him added moral stature, and he inspired the Janata coalition in 1977. The victory of that coalition in the elections led to a reaffirmation of Gandhism as the ideology of the Indian state under Morarji Desai. Thirty years after the Mahatma's death, Gandhian ideas inspired the coalition which, for the first time, defeated the Congress Party, ironically the very party that had been Gandhi's own creation.

One of the outcomes of the JP phase was the political re-emergence of the Hindu Right, which had played a major role in the anti-Indira coalition. Outwardly it rallied to 'Gandhian socialism', which its ideological mentor Savarkar had always fought against. But this reversal of its policies was more apparent than real. What the Janata government of 1977 showed above all was that Gandhian ideas had become the common property of the Indian political class and were in danger of losing their emancipatory content. This was the more so when JP, the 'keeper of the temple', died in 1980 and left no heir. With JP's death it could be said that Gandhi's direct posthumous political trajectory had come to an end. Following the disappearance of the generation of those who had known him (although Vinoba Bhave continued his increasingly solitary campaign for Bhoodan till his death), his presence was felt in a much more indirect way. While all Indian political parties, both of the Right and the Left, claim Gandhi as an inspiration, it has not prevented them supporting, from 1991 onwards, a programme of economic liberalization which is a clear departure from the economic nationalism that was the core element in Gandhi's thought. The Gandhian reference in India is more and more devoid of specific content. Although Gandhi remains a legitimizing image that no group or individual can dispense with, the more one tends to pay tribute to him the less his message is taken seriously.

It is mostly among the many NGOs and environmentalists that serious reflection is carried out as to the ways in which it is possible to adapt Gandhi's thought and teachings to the challenges of the contemporary world. While there are no direct heirs to Gandhi, there is a whole milieu of activists who claim inspiration from him. Some of them continue to call themselves Gandhians and refer to a doctrine—which remains often vague and ill-defined. Despite his refusal to espouse a doctrine, Gandhi is seen by many as an important political thinker.

Gandhism and Its Interpreters

Gandhi never claimed he was the founder of a political or religious doctrine. He was an enemy of all 'isms' and more generally of all systems. Apart from *Hind Swaraj*, written in 1909, he left no theoretical text and expressed himself mainly through press articles and occasional pamphlets hastily written in the midst of political and social activity. The enormous amount of writing gathered in the *Collected Works* consists mainly of correspondence relating to varied topics (diet is one of the most widely represented), as well as transcriptions of speeches and addresses. It is difficult to extract the outlines of a coherent doctrine from such a jumble. Many, however, have not shirked from attempting to do this, during Gandhi's lifetime and even more so following his death. In many Indian universities there are chairs of

Gandhian thought and journals are specifically devoted to his teachings. The idea has gained acceptance that his thought formed something of a system, which has been often called 'Gandhism'. Although the exact origins of the use of this term are difficult to trace—it would appear to have been used for the first time by Philip Spratt, an English ex-communist, in a book entitled *Gandhism: An Analysis*[6]—it became current from the 1940s—in 1940 Nirmal Kumar Bose, a close associate of Gandhi, published his *Studies in Gandhism*.[7] The term is used concurrently with expressions such as 'Gandhian thought' and 'Gandhian ideas'. While several organizations calling themselves 'Gandhian' were created in India in the 1950s, that curious artefact, Gandhism, became a staple offering on the market of political doctrines. At some stage, it was seen as an antidote to Marxism (another posthumous invention), but it has apparently better resisted wear and tear than its rival. Gandhism presents itself not as a formal doctrine but a loose collection of terms which are supposed to define the main outlines of Gandhi's political thought and action. Terms such as *ahimsa*, satyagraha, sarvodaya, *swadeshi* and swaraj are probably the most common of these, the first two referring to non-violence, the third to Gandhi's economic doctrine, the fourth to his economic nationalism, and the fifth to his notion of India's political independence.

Before the 1970s, Gandhism had been seen mostly as a doctrine of non-violence. But, paradoxically, Gandhi himself did not write extensively about it, or at least he did not produce any general treatise which could be used as a guide for action. On the other hand, commentators on Gandhi have written a lot about it. In Gandhi's lifetime Richard Gregg, an American lawyer trained in Harvard who stayed in India between 1925 and 1930 and who spent some time in Gandhi's ashram, published *The Power of Non-Violence*,[8] a book which had a considerable impact in the English-speaking world, including India. Nehru saw it as the most successful attempt at giving 'scientific' shape to the doctrine of non-violence. Gregg developed a sophisticated argument for non-violence, making use of social science and psychology. He used a metaphor, 'moral jiu-jitsu', to define the ability of non-violent resistance to destabilize the adversary. His influence on

[6] P. Spratt, *Gandhism: An Analysis*, Madras, 1939.
[7] N.K. Bose, *Studies in Gandhism*, Calcutta, 1940.
[8] R. Gregg, *The Power of Non-Violence*, Philadelphia, 1934.

the American Civil Rights Movement was significant, and it was partly through his book that Gandhi's teachings became known to many Americans.

After Gandhi's death, a growing body of literature came out on this subject. It generally combined the study of some of Gandhi's texts, often selected in a somewhat arbitrary fashion, and an analysis of some of the movements he led or inspired. This is particularly so in Joan Bondurant's book, *Conquest of Violence*,[9] probably the most systematic attempt at deriving a philosophy for the resolution of conflicts from Gandhi. Bondurant left aside Gandhi's South African campaigns and focused on the practice of satyagraha in India between 1917 and 1930. She started with a definition of some basic principles underpinning satyagraha, particularly the search for truth and the notion of non-violence as ahimsa, which Gandhi identified, *de facto*, with love. According to Bondurant's interpretation, non-violent action was for Gandhi the only test of truth. She then tried to analyse how these principles were put into effect in a series of movements. There was also in her book an attempt at evaluating the innovations Gandhi brought about in relation to 'Hindu tradition'—which she defined rather normatively. She examined Gandhi's position *vis-à-vis* such political labels as 'conservative' and 'anarchist' to conclude that his method transcended such labels and was compatible with all of them. She ended with an analysis of 'Gandhian dialectics' which, according to her, did not aim simply at limiting violence, but sought to eradicate it durably. She saw Gandhi as a 'rational utopian' whose methods offered a possible way of fighting 'totalitarian' regimes. Bondurant's inspiration from Hannah Arendt is evident and the book reflects a phase in the history of American political philosophy.

After Bondurant, other American authors on non-violence inspired by Gandhi's ideas have been Gene Sharp, whose book *The Politics of Nonviolent Action*[10] is probably the most systematic theoretical elaboration of the question; Mark Juergensmeyer;[11] and Dennis Dalton.[12]

[9] J. Bondurant, *Conquest of Violence: The Gandhian Philosophy of Violence*, Princeton, 1st edn, 1958.

[10] G. Sharp, *The Politics of Nonviolent Action*, Boston, 1973.

[11] M. Juergensmeyer, *Fighting with Gandhi*, New York, 1984.

[12] D. Dalton, *Mahatma Gandhi: Nonviolent Power in Action*, New York, 1993.

The particular fascination of American authors for this aspect of Gandhi's thought and action can be explained by the existence of specific interrogations in America regarding the use of violence in politics, in part triggered by the struggle of Afro-Americans against racial oppression. The impact of Gandhi's ideas on non-violence was, however, felt well beyond the United States.

Leaving aside theoretical works, two different but not contradictory readings of Gandhian non-violence have also been developed outside India. In the first reading, Gandhi's teaching is seen as offering an array of techniques to fight situations of oppression without resorting to armed violence. The second reading extends the application of the Gandhian doctrine to the field of international relations, seeing in it the first lineaments of a 'peace science' necessary to oppose the menace of nuclear warfare.

Leaders of various anti-colonialist and anti-racist movements were inspired by the example of India's Gandhian independence struggle (or at least by the idealized image they had of it) and tried to apply Gandhian methods in different situations of struggle. The two most remarkable cases are those of the American Civil Rights Movement and the anti-apartheid struggle in South Africa. It is easy to understand why those two countries proved particularly favourable to the develop-ment of non-violent movements on the Gandhian model. The situa-tions of racial oppression which they faced lent themselves well to the use of these methods, which of course Gandhi had first applied in South Africa. It must be added that both movements had a Protestant leadership which felt special affinities with Gandhi and operated with-in the largely British legal system that had existed in India. The deve-lopment of mass non-violent movements in both countries closely recalled some of Gandhi's satyagraha campaigns. Their leaders, Albert Luthuli and Martin Luther King, consciously modelled themselves on Gandhi.

However, a close reading of Martin Luther King's own narrative shows that he placed Gandhi within a continuum, linking the civil rights movement to the passive resistance of early Christians, as well as to the fight of American settlers against the British; King did not give Gandhi a foundational status. He became aware of Gandhi at an early stage in his career and described the influence the Mahatma had on him: 'The moral and intellectual satisfaction which I could not derive from Bentham and Mill's utilitarianism, from Marx and Lenin's revolutionary methods, from Hobbes' theory of social contract, from Rousseau's optimism of "return to nature", from Nietzsche's philosophy of superman, I found in the philosophy of non-violent resistance of Gandhi.'[13] But he took care to replace the fight for civil rights within a more specifically American and Christian cultural context. In his autobiography, when speaking of the fight against segregation in buses in Montgomery, he emphasized the synthesis between the 'Christian doctrine of love' and 'the Gandhian method of nonviolence'. After mentioning a letter by a white sympathizer of the movement to a local newspaper, in which an explicit comparison was drawn between the boycott of buses in Montgomery and Gandhi's struggle in India, King wrote:

> in the summer of 1957 the name of Mahatma Gandhi was well known in Montgomery. People who had never heard of the little brown saint of India were now saying his name with an air of familiarity. Nonviolent resistance had emerged as the technique of the movement, while love stood as the regulating idea. In other words, Christ furnished the spirit and motivation while Gandhi furnished the method.[14]

The attempt to limit Gandhi to the role of simple provider of a method can be explained by the specific social and ideological context in which King had to operate. He sought to mobilize a population for whom the only meaningful references were biblical ones, and he also wanted to remain within an American framework so as to make the struggle clear to the white population. This prevented him from giving Gandhi too definite a role as a source of inspiration. On the other hand, King's narrative does show to what extent he was influenced by Gandhi, not only in the method of the struggle but also in its content:

[13] King discovered Gandhi while studying theology, when he heard a sermon by Reverend Mordecai Johnson, the president of Howard University, who had met Gandhi in the course of a trip to India with a delegation of black American intellectuals in 1936. He was so taken up with Gandhi that he started devouring books about him. See Clayborne Carson (ed.), *The Autobiography of Martin Luther King Jr*, London, 1999, pp. 23–4.

[14] Ibid., p. 67.

Like their predecessors, the Black Americans were ready to risk martyrdom so as to shake and move the social conscience of their community
and of the entire nation. Instead of submitting to the covert cruelty that
manifests itself in thousands of jails and in many dark street corners, they
wanted to force their opponents to display overtly their brutality, in full
daylight, in the face of the whole world . . .

This is typical Gandhian reasoning about the necessity of suffering to
influence an opponent to give in. Recourse to mass imprisonment was
also a typically Gandhian device. King relied more, however, for the
purpose of mobilizing his constituency, on his oratory, which was by
all accounts much superior to Gandhi's.

In South Africa, the Gandhian filiation of the movement was even
more direct. The African National Congress, which in 1952 launched the first mass movement against apartheid under the leadership of
Dr Albert Luthuli,[15] had been founded in 1912 on the model of the
Natal Indian Congress, with which Gandhi had been closely associated.
The movement used civil disobedience and boycott, but the white
powers were not impressed and it is well known that, following mass
arrests and trials in the early 1960s, the ANC chose to combine mass
resistance with forms of armed struggle. In his autobiography, Nelson
Mandela, while paying tribute to Gandhi and his role in South Africa,
criticized non-violent methods.[16]

Non-violent methods of struggle were also used in the more familiar context of anti-colonial movements, particularly in Africa. Two
African leaders who claimed inspiration from Gandhi were Kwame
Nkrumah in the Gold Coast, who was doubly influenced by Marxism
and Gandhism, and Kenneth Kaunda in North Rhodesia. Kaunda in
particular called himself a disciple of Gandhi,[17] and mass non-violent
agitation played an important role in the decolonization process in
Central Africa.

In the 1950s and 1960s, the impact of Gandhian ideas was felt well
beyond the United States and the colonized world. Among movements

[15] See A. Luthuli, *Let My People Go*, New York, London, 1962.

[16] N. Mandela, *No Easy Walk to Freedom*, London, 1965 (1st edn), pp. 110–
21.

[17] K. Kaunda, *Zambia shall be Free: An Autobiography*, London, Ibadan,
Nairobi, 1962.

which betrayed some Gandhian influence, Danilo Dolci's fight against poverty and the Mafia in Sicily deserve mention. Dolci seems to have discovered independently some of the basic principles of non-violent struggle; later the reference to Gandhi was used explicitly by him, but it remained a general inspiration rather than a very characterized influence.[18] One could also mention, in the French context, Lanza del Vasto and his community of the Arch, which launched struggles against the Algerian War in the 1960s and against the extension of a military camp in the 1970s (in which the anti-globalization activist José Bové had his training). These were never, however, mass struggles, and mobilized mostly small groups of activists.

In the field of international relations, the most sytematic attempt at extending the application of Gandhian ideas was Arne Naess's programme of 'non-violent national defence' aimed at defusing nuclear conflict.[19] Following Naess, the anti-nuclear movement of the 1960s often invoked the Mahatma as an inspiration.

Gandhi and Political Philosophy

In the 1970s there occurred a clear shift in perception, as Gandhi started being taken more seriously as a political philosopher and thinker, beyond his contribution to the theory of non-violence, and as the interrelation between various aspects of this thought received more emphasis. In 1971, when John Rawls published his classic *Theory of Justice*,[20] his discussion of civil disobedience ignored Gandhi's contribution altogether. The renewed interest in Gandhi as a political philosopher was mainly initiated by Indian academics who had settled abroad and occupied a relatively marginal position in the discipline. Two major attempts to appraise Gandhi's contribution to political

[18] On Dolci, see M. Bess, 'Peace Through Social Transformation: Danilo Dolci's Long-Range Experiments with Gandhian Nonviolence', in M. Bess, *Realism, Utopia and the Mushroom Cloud: Four Activist Intellectuals and their Strategies for Peace, 1945–1989*, Chicago and London, 1993, pp. 155–217.

[19] A. Naess, *Gandhi and the Nuclear Age*, Totowa (NJ), 1965.

[20] J. Rawls, *A Theory of Justice*, Cambridge, Mass., 1971. On differences between Rawls' and Gandhi's notions of civil disobedience, see V. Haksar, *Civil Disobedience: Threats and Offers (Gandhi and Rawls)*, Oxford and New York, 1986.

philosophy were those by Raghavan Iyer, an Indian academic working in the US, in his book published in 1973,[21] and by Bhiku Parekh, a British academic of Indian origin, in a 1989 publication.[22]

Iyer deplored, in the preface of his book, the fact that in spite of the abundance of books written about Gandhi, 'scant justice [had] been done to the solid conceptual foundations of his thought'.[23] He proposed to leave aside the question whether Gandhi was a saint or a politician and to take as a point of departure the idea that he was, above all, preoccupied with truth. He based his analysis upon the study of a number of key notions and tried to delineate interrelations between them, in particular the central relationship between truth and non-violence. Regarding the crucial question of the relationship between ends and means, he stressed similarities between the thought of Gandhi and the thought of the Catholic philosopher Jacques Maritain, both rejecting absolutely the possibility that questionable means could lead to a morally desirable end. Although he was not unaware of the existence of contradictions in Gandhi's thought, Iyer wanted to emphasize its overall coherence and prophetic aspects. He tried to situate Gandhi within a tradition of 'classical' political thought going back to Plato and tended to underline the normative rather than the pragmatic side of his teachings.

The merit of Parekh's book is to put forward a critical appreciation of Gandhi's political thought—which is largely absent in Iyer's. Parekh sees in Gandhi a profound, but at the same time limited, political thinker. According to him, Gandhi's great strength lies in his analysis of the role of morality in politics, which allows him to go beyond anthropocentrism and ground political anthropology in the world of nature, taking into account the 'ecological' dimension. This is a clear instance of the influence of contemporary political trends on a reading of Gandhi. For the same author, Gandhi's central weakness is his epistemology, particularly his extreme methodological individualism, which leads him to accord legitimacy to any point of view provided it is sincere. This results in a kind of aporia, for it becomes

[21] R.N. Iyer, *The Moral and Political Thought of Mahatma Gandhi*, op. cit.

[22] B. Parekh, *Gandhi's Political Philosophy: A Critical Examination*, Basingstoke, 1989.

[23] R.N. Iyer, *The Moral and Political Thought of Mahatma Gandhi*, op. cit., p. IX.

impossible to differentiate between different viewpoints on the basis of their ethical validity.

In India, there arose in the 1980s a lively intellectual debate around Gandhi. A group of authors, whom one could call 'nativist', proposed a new reading of Gandhi which gave pride of place to his critique of modernity. Ashis Nandy's work is the most well-known instance of this trend, which has been extremely influential in India. Nandy sees Gandhi as a hero of cultural resistance to colonialism: 'It was colonial India, still preserving something of its androgynous cosmology and style, which ultimately produced a transcultural protest against the hyper-masculine world view of colonialism, in the form of Gandhi . . .'[24] This interpretation of Gandhi as a kind of cultural hero rather than a systematic thinker became popular because here Gandhi's inability to develop a coherent system of thought is seen in a positive light. For Nandy, Gandhi was representative of an Indian, or rather Hindu, communitarian conscience whose logic was basically opposed to Western modernity. He views identifications of Gandhi with modern Indian nationalism as a hegemonic act of appropriation perpetrated by the Indian state in its quest for legitimacy, an act which denies the profound meaning of the Gandhian message.

This conception of Gandhi became popular in intellectual circles attracted to alternative ideologies, but it met with opposition among Indian intellectuals who situated themselves, in one way or another, within a Marxist framework. For the latter, Gandhi was basically a figure in the transition of India towards a bourgeois or capitalistic modernity, in spite of his proclaimed opposition to it. A good example of this trend is to be found in the work by Ravinder Kumar, one of India's foremost historians. On the basis of the notion of 'epochal hero', Kumar draws a parallel between the Buddha and Gandhi: while the former exemplified the entry of India into agrarian civilization, Gandhi symbolized its entry into bourgeois modernity, understood as a global process, encompassing the social, political and cultural fields.[25] He sees Gandhi's role as a link between the élite and the masses through the method of satyagraha. In the face of objections from those

[24] A. Nandy, *The Intimate Enemy: Loss and Recovery of Self under Colonialism*, Delhi, 1983, p. 48.

[25] R. Kumar, 'Gandhi and India's Transition to Bourgeois Modernity', in *Addressing Gandhi*, New Delhi, 1995, pp. 25–32.

who underlined the traditional aspect of Gandhi's ideas, he puts forward the idea of a 'strategic' use of tradition to achieve aims which were, ultimately, modern.

Recent re-evaluations of Gandhi owe a lot to ongoing paradigmatic shifts in the field of political philosophy, and more generally the social sciences. But the more direct influence of political change is also perceptible. It is difficult to avoid the thought that the elevation of Gandhism into a system of thought had to do with attempts at finding a 'third way' between capitalism and communism, such as flourished at a certain stage in the Cold War. Since the 1970s, Gandhi has been seen by many mainly as a forerunner of ecology and alternative movements.

Gandhi, Political Ecology, and Alternative Movements

With the advent of the so-called economic crisis of the early 1970s, there was an upsurge in readings of Gandhi as the formulator of an economic programme which was an alternative to liberal capitalism. The publication by Ernst Schumacher in 1973 of his cult book, *Small is Beautiful*,[26] refocused attention on the idea of 'appropriate technology' which was already present in an embryonic state in Gandhi's programme for the development of village industries. Although Schumacher himself was more influenced by Buddhist thought and his own experience in Burma, there were obvious similarities between his ideas and those of Gandhi. There developed, therefore, a new reading of Gandhi as an 'ecological' thinker, culminating in 1987 with the well-known report of the Bruntlandt Commission on the future of mankind, which openly acknowledged its Gandhian inspiration. In India, the ecological movements which developed in the wake of the 1973 'Chipko Andolan' agitation for the safeguard of Himalayan forests also invoked Gandhi's name. The complexity of the relationship between Indian ecological movements and Gandhi is brought out by Ramachandra Guha.[27] While reaffirming that 'Gandhi has been

[26] E.F. Schumacher, *Small is Beautiful. A Study of Economics as if People Mattered*, London, 1973.

[27] R. Guha, 'Gandhi and the Environmental Movement', *An Anthropologist Among the Marxists and Other Essays*, Delhi, 2001.

the patron saint, generally acknowledged, sometimes rejected, of the Indian ecological movement', he distinguishes between Gandhi's direct intellectual influence, which he finds limited, and a more indirect influence on the methods of struggle. On the first point, he stresses some of the limitations in Gandhi's thought concerning, in particular, the urban question and the 'wild'—two major preoccupations among contemporary ecologists. Guha gives greater importance in the genesis of the movement to J.C. Kumarappa, a close disciple of Gandhi, whom he views as 'the first Indian ecologist'. Gandhi's influence was more perceptible at the level of the methods of struggle: most ecological movements tried to use methods of non-violent mass resistance to achieve their objectives, with varying degrees of success.

Green movements outside India have also claimed an affinity with Gandhi. In Germany, an important leader of the Green Party, Petra Kelly, wrote in the early 1990s that the Green Party had been directly influenced by Gandhi in thinking that 'a lifestyle and a method of production which rely on an endless supply of raw materials and a lavish use of these raw materials generates the motive for the violent appropriation of raw materials from other countries'.[28] Despite such attempts at linking ecological struggle to a precise theme in Gandhi's writings, for the younger generations in the West, the dominant image of the Mahatma is that of a kind of ancestor of ecology and alternative politics. This perception is not necessarily based upon a precise knowledge of his thought and action. His presence is more that of an icon than a really inspiring ideologue.

From the time of his stay in South Africa, Gandhi became a public figure constantly open to public scrutiny. He wrote a lot, laying himself open to the judgement of posterity. The extraordinary diversity of images of Gandhi in his lifetime is partly the result of this openness. There are few public figures among Gandhi's contemporaries, in India and abroad, who have not at some point had something to say about him. A collection of their statements would fill several thick volumes. Posterity has been more selective. Of the many pronouncements made about Gandhi, it has chosen to retain mainly those which tend towards

[28] Petra K. Kelly, 'Gandhi and the Green Party', in S. Mukherjee and S. Ramaswamy (eds), *Facets of Mahatma Gandhi*, vol. 1, New Delhi, 1994, pp. 341–54.

the hagiographical. The picture of Gandhi resulting from this selection is very biased. What is missing is precisely what made him such a radiant figure, the charm laced with humour which captivated those who met him; what remains are the austerities of the saint, and his highest meditations on God and ethics. Also missing is what made Gandhi's daily routine—the meticulous attention to mundane tasks, the shopkeeper's mentality which led him to count and recount, the obsession with parsimony and saving a few pies. These manifestations of his social origins in a milieu of the merchant caste and the strong influence of Victorian Protestant values made Gandhi the man. To recapture the historical Gandhi behind the Gandhi of the legend, the man behind the icon, the leader behind the saint, a very down-to-earth perspective needs to be adopted, and much attention must be paid to the context.

PART TWO
Gandhi in History

CHAPTER 4

Birth of a Leader

F ocusing on perceptions of Gandhi has left us with a fragmented
landscape, a kind of puzzle which has to be reassembled, not to
give an idea of coherence, but to draw attention to the many questions left pending. These concern mainly Gandhi's entry into public
life, first in the context of South Africa and second in India during the
years 1915–20 which saw his rise to the position of prime leader of
the Indian nationalist movement. Gandhi was literally a twice-born
leader: the organizer of the South African struggle had to go through
a further transformation before emerging at the head of India's struggle for freedom. The experience of South Africa was decisive, a point
too often lost on Gandhi's biographers.

Private Life, Public Life

For Gandhi, private life and public life were one and the same. From
the time he was constantly in the public eye, he never sought to preserve a private domain. He lived his life in full sight and hearing of all,
in a kind of absolute transparence. The ethical rules he followed in his
private life were those he wanted to apply in public life. Public and
private were not separate spheres but a continuum, linking the biologi-
cal family to the nation, an intermediary stage being the spiritual
'enlarged family' which was the ashram. Across the whole of this space,
the same ethical rules applied. It was not a normative view; Gandhi did
not specifically argue that a leader had to behave in the same way in
public as in private. His point was rather that any fault in a man's private behaviour had inevitable repercussions in his public behaviour,
inasmuch as the two could not be separated. So the study of Gandhi's
public career cannot be divorced from an analysis of his private life.

In this sense, Erikson's insight is indeed profound, and his analysis of the 1918 strike in Ahmedabad throws interesting light on the nature of the Gandhian leadership. However, Erikson's strictures on Gandhi as a father and a husband, though easy enough to share, are less helpful. In any case Gandhi's conception of public life as a total commitment was not easily compatible with the pursuit of a 'normal' family life.

Gandhi's radical indictment of human sexuality, except as a purely reproductive function (with many caveats thrown in) is obviously excessive, but in the Indian context some merit may be recognized in his plea for detachment *vis-à-vis* family ties. Given the weight of family and caste in India, the fact that Gandhi had renounced both gave him an aura which undoubtedly helped him in his career. Since this renunciation occurred gradually during the South African years, it is necessary to look closely at this period.

The Contribution of South Africa

Most biographers treat the South African period, at least implicitly, in a teleological fashion, as a simple preparation to Gandhi's later emergence in India as a nationalist leader. They seem to think that Gandhi blossomed fully only in India and suggest that there was something preordained about his eventual return there. On the other hand, keeping contingency in mind, one could choose to present the South African episode as a kind of separate life, with its own logic, and not necessarily as a preparation for what followed. The most fruitful approach seems to be to use that episode as a key to an understanding of Gandhi's political personality, and of the way in which it developed. The mystery is, as I said, how Gandhi, an intensely private and shy young man, transformed himself into a public figure, a leader of men, recognized in 1913–14 as an interlocutor by both the South African premier and the viceroy of India. The exact genesis of such a complete transformation taxes the ingenuity of even the most perspicacious biographer.

In South Africa, a context described by Gandhi as well as commentators and later historians as oppressive for Indians, Gandhi blossomed in a way he could probably not have had he stayed on in Rajkot. The paradox demands an explanation which no existing biography offers.

Gandhi's success in his legal career deserves far more notice, but it seems writers prefer not to dwell on it because it does not conform to the stereotype of the renouncer. Around 1905–6 Gandhi's legal practice in Johannesburg fetched him an annual income of £ 5000, a considerable sum at the time. It is therefore most likely that Gandhi's lack of interest in money in later years was less a 'natural' cast of mind than a deliberate choice. We may surmise that Gandhi's success in his professional career was not without impact upon the substantial development of his personality, endowing him with a self-confidence he completely lacked earlier. The financial aspect of his career deserves attention at least for what it reveals about Gandhi's capacities. Sometimes it is argued that Gandhi, being about the only Indian lawyer in South Africa, deserves no great credit for his success. But his success was not evident at the outset. When he arrived in South Africa, Gandhi had a purely bookish knowledge of the law and was ignorant of commercial law, mastery of which was indispensable in a milieu of merchants. After a few years he acquired the reputation of being a competent as well as honest lawyer. He obtained regular custom from merchants who, before his arrival, had used the services of European lawyers. Gandhi also earned a measure of respect from his European colleagues, which, in as profoundly racist a society as colonial South Africa in the late nineteenth century, was no mean achievement. He acquired skills which were to keep him in good stead in his future career in politics: he learnt how to prepare a brief, how to question witnesses, how to plead a cause. This learning involved a sort of sheer obstinacy, for he does not appear to have been gifted with any particular talent for oratory. His ability to focus on the task reveals he was not devoid of worldly ambition, at least in so far as this was not incompatible with a desire to serve the cause of his compatriots in South Africa.

In his *Autobiography*, Gandhi summarized his South African years: 'I had gone to South Africa to travel, to escape the intrigues of Kathiawar and to earn a living. But, as I said, I found myself in search of God and engaged in a quest of self-realization.' The first part of the sentence is a frank admission of the real reasons for his departure, which were essentially financial; the second part brings in the spiritual dimension and tends to suggest that Gandhi was motivated by a force greater than himself. As we have already seen, the transformation he underwent was not due only to a spiritual crisis. In the dynamics of action, the future Mahatma was led to seek a different kind of relationship with his fel-low countrymen, particularly rich merchants. To be recognized by them as a leader, rather than simply as a representative, he had to acquire cultural capital—which could be only of a symbolic nature. Celibacy and conversion to a simple life were two devices through which he tried to acquire this symbolic capital; it earned him the respect of his merchant friends. It would seem that spiritual maturation and political necessities went hand in hand.

What can be conjectured is that, by the time he moved to Johannesburg, Gandhi had fulfilled the initial programme he had set out for himself on his arrival in South Africa. The shy young lawyer had become *somebody*, a respected member of the Indian community in South Africa and recognized as such by the colonial authorities. He had also succeeded in earning the respect, even the friendship, of a few white men and women. It is not coincidence that, in his *Autobiography*, Gandhi devotes two full pages to Miss Schlesin,[1] his European secretary in his legal practice at Johannesburg, stressing her exceptional devotion to him. For the Western reader today, this evocation is simply supplementary proof of Gandhi's radiance, of his capacity to instil devotion in others, especially women. But, for an Indian reader in the 1920s the text probably carried a different connotation. It was very rare for an Indian at the time (with the exception of maharajahs) to employ Europeans, especially female Europeans, and this reversal of accepted norms no doubt enhanced Gandhi's status in the eyes of his readers. What this particular bit of information reveals is that, as far as social and professional success was concerned, Gandhi had reached the top of what an Indian in South Africa could aspire to. Gandhi, however, influenced by Ruskin and Tolstoi, as well as by his own religious maturation, had higher aspirations: he wanted to exercise true moral leadership over his fellow countrymen, whom he found apathetic.

The South African period was thus doubly crucial in the development of Gandhi's personality. It transformed a shy youth into a confident leader, capable of daring initiative. It also transformed a loyal subject

---

[1] Gandhi, *Autobiography*, op. cit., pp. 236–7.

of the British empire, apparently not much concerned with politics, into an Indian patriot.

Gandhi's transformation into a public figure necessitated the acquisition of literary competence, for he never became a great orator. His unprepossessing physique handicapped him, his voice was not sonorous, he lacked an imposing presence. He did not show much interest in mastering the laws of rhetoric, whether in Gujarati or in English, and always expressed himself simply, in the manner of a teacher. His style of writing was conversational. His political schooling came through journalism, which he started with *Indian Opinion* and continued via *Harijan* and *Navajivan*. He practised a form of journalism decidedly didactic. He used the medium of the press to educate readers rather than comment on current events. He invented a style of journalism entirely his own, and it remained till the end of his life an important facet of his activity. There was no stylistic refinement in his writings; he sought to captivate readers through a very direct form of address.

In South Africa he also learnt how to give interviews, and more generally how to deal with the media, a skill which he used all his life to great effect. He now also acquired the social competence he sorely lacked; he overcame his shyness, addressed crowds, and developed argumentative skills. He showed an ability to form lasting friendships, beyond racial barriers, with Indians and Europeans. (It has been remarked, however, that in South Africa he had no African friends.) He acquired, in fact, European friends who remained close to him till the end of his life—men like C.F. Andrews, Polak and Kallenbach, all of whom had strong personalities but were socially fairly marginal. Gandhi was good at mobilizing them in the defence of his cause, and he started developing a special gift for drawing towards himself talented but slightly marginal individuals. In South Africa he embarked on a voyage of self-discovery which allowed him to realize that he had a lot of hidden talents.

Why did he have to cross the oceans to be able to discover himself? Although it may appear paradoxical, Gandhi's construction of his Indianness was an outcome of his South African stay. Little is known of the way in which he defined himself at the time of his arrival in the colony, beyond the fact that he prided himself on being a loyal subject of the British empire. From 1906, there is no doubt he saw himself primarily as an Indian patriot. The specific circumstances of South Africa played a major role in enhancing his feeling of being Indian. Apart from the usual nostalgia bred of exile, Gandhi felt strongly about the oppression to which Indians were subject, their constant harassment by white settlers and the colonial authorities, all of which he deemed contrary to his own utopian ideals of imperial brotherhood. Gandhi's vision of India broadened now, and he embraced even humble coolies as fellow countrymen: this would have been more difficult in India, where social barriers between the upper and lower castes were still unbreachable.

This sort of emergence of Gandhi's Indianness did not imply his denial of other identities. Gandhi had some feeling, however ill-defined, of belonging to a Hindu community, without hostility to Muslims, whom he saw as compatriots. His position as spokesman for a largely Muslim merchant grouping did not breed resentment; on the contrary he felt a particular closeness to them, even if this did not extend into a deep understanding of their religion. He was aware of religious differences between Hindus and Muslims, which he found impossible to overcome. In a letter to a nephew who wanted to get married he wrote: 'If the husband and wife belong to different religions, there can be no sense of oneness.'[2] His relationship to the Hindu community, however, remained fairly loose; he never belonged to any of the existing sects, and kept his distance from the Arya Samaj, which was influential in South Africa. Nor did his Gujarati provincial patriotism, deeply felt as it was, come in the way of his interaction with Indians of other provinces. He made much effort to develop links with Tamils and Telugus, who formed the bulk of the coolie class in South Africa. He tried, even if rather unsuccessfully, to learn their languages and understand their culture and customs.

His Indian patriotism coexisted with a strong feeling of imperial patriotism. He never missed an opportunity to express admiration for the British constitution, in which he saw an unrivalled charter of freedom. He always stood up to listen to the national anthem, and prior to 1920 showed himself a loyal subject of the Crown. These two forms

[2] Letter to Jamnadas Gandhi, 19 July 1913, *The Collected Works of Mahatma Gandhi*, op. cit., vol. 12, p. 147.

of patriotism did not at this time appear to him antithetical. Inasmuch as he considered India's place in the British empire as the best guarantee of Indian rights all over the empire, his loyalism, which was never a feeling of loyalty towards the person of the sovereign but was strongly based on principle, did not seem incompatible with Indian patriotism. For him, being a Hindu, a Gujarati, a subject of the empire, all contributed to making him an Indian patriot.

His patriotism, from 1909, assumed an increasingly messianic dimension. Gandhi saw himself endowed with a mission in relation to India. Once he had discovered the weapon of satyagraha, he appears to have broadened his political horizon to think in terms of a political career in India. In *Hind Swaraj*, which he wrote in 1909 on the ship which took him back from England to South Africa, his object was the political future of India. In spite of his long stay in South Africa, he did not become a South African Indian, his vision remained directed towards his native land. A contributing factor was probably that, though he took his family to South Africa, from a certain point in time he eschewed 'normal' family life. The experiments with communal living that he carried out first in Phoenix, and later in Tolstoi Farm, played a major role in shaping his public life. They allowed him to distance himself from his immediate family to embrace a broader concept of family life, better suited to his peripatetic lifestyle and aspirations. Around 1909, he was, in the way described in Doke's book, an 'Indian patriot in South Africa'. Between 1909 and 1914 South Africa for him was a kind of laboratory, a field for experiment. He tried some of his ideas and refined the new method of political struggle that he had chanced upon. Although he was loath to admit it, he nurtured growing political ambitions. He developed close links with one of Congress's major leaders, Gokhale, whose visit to South Africa he organized in 1912. Later, he would present himself as Gokhale's political heir. All this was not purely contingent, contrary to his way of presenting it—even if it did not fall into a coherent strategy.

In his autobiography Gandhi sought, more or less consciously, to give the impression that he was foreign to any political ambition, that he chanced upon politics while engaged on a spiritual quest. This sounds very much like *ex post facto* rationalization. There are many indications that, around forty, Gandhi, in spite of his professional success, went through a kind of existential crisis and sought to give his life a new meaning. He saw public service as the only way forward and formed the project of embarking upon a political career in India. Conditions not being favourable to his immediate return, he launched himself into large-scale struggles in South Africa, awaiting more favourable circumstances in India. When he eventually returned he was a man whose only spiritual allegiance was to India: he had no family, no caste, no community. The breach with caste began when he left for England, and it became final with his departure for South Africa. Gandhi was in fact a man without a caste, without a *jati*, even if he believed in the hierarchy of *varna*. In South Africa Gandhi was at the same time uprooted and rooted anew: he lost his family and his caste but he became an Indian.

It could almost be said that, when he came back to India in 1915, he was one of a kind there. His compatriots defined themselves primarily in terms of their family and caste, then of their religion and their region of origin, and their Indianness was only the last layer, the most superficial one, in this layered identity. In Gandhi's case, his Indian identity had precedence over his Hindu and Gujarati identity. So, this exemplary citizen of the British empire really discovered his Indianness in South Africa, through the experience of exile and oppression. This is not unique: other examples which come to mind are those of Irish nationalism developing in exile in America and England, or Herzl discovering his Jewishness in Paris at the time of the Dreyfus affair, and one could draw from such examples a poetics of exile and uprooting. But with Gandhi India was more a home of the spirit than of the flesh.

If by 1915 Gandhi was clearly an Indian patriot, was he already at that time an Indian nationalist? There is no easy answer to the question. If nationalism meant an aggressive assertion of identity, Gandhi was not a nationalist: his conception of India's political future was still firmly situated within the framework of the British empire, as it was for Gokhale and the Congress moderates. If nationalism was taken in a more precise political sense, as a demand for greater autonomy for India within the empire, then Gandhi was a nationalist. But he was still largely an outsider in India's political life. He had no regional constituency, an essential asset for a political career in India at the time.

Nor had he a programme, for in spite of his closeness to Gokhale, he did not share the latter's deep insights into institutional politics. Nor did Gandhi have a method, being well aware that satyagraha as defined in the South African context could not be applied in India without adjustment and fine-tuning.

In 1915–20, he pursued three major objectives: to acquire a political base, to forge a programme, and to adapt satyagraha to the Indian context.

The Emergence of a National Leader in 1915–20

Between 1915 and 1920 Gandhi had to literally reinvent himself so as to be able to play the political role he had had in mind since 1909. To move from leadership of the South African struggle to leader of the Indian people's struggle implied a change of scale and perspective. It took Gandhi five years to accomplish this. The change of scale was momentous: there were 300,000 Indians in South Africa, in India there were 300 million. Whereas the South African Indian population was fairly diverse in terms of religion and ethnicity, it was nothing compared to the heterogeneity of India's population. In South Africa, the situation of the Indians as an oppressed minority created strong bonds between them and made it possible to overcome barriers of caste and religion. In India, while Indians shared the feeling of being oppressed, there were enormous differences between them. In 1915, there was no single demand on which they could unite against British rule. Only repression in Punjab in 1919 offered a truly national cause. Gandhi, however, had to go through the detour of supporting a more specific cause—that of the Khilafat—to reach the position of national leader.

More fundamentally, the shift from South Africa to India demanded a huge change in Gandhi's political perspective and language. In South Africa he had pursued limited aims centred around winning those elementary rights which, on paper, were the due of all subjects of the empire: Gandhi was able to exploit the gap which existed between British political norms and the actual situation of Indians. His political language was that of rights in an imperial context. To wrest these he had been innovative, but now he could not merely denounce the contrast between an imperial norm and political reality. He had to invent a whole new vocabulary. Gandhi did not immediately become aware of the exigencies of the situation. For a few years, he tried to cling to the imperial idiom; only in 1920 did he renounce it once and for all. Over the years 1915–20, Gandhi learnt to operate in the Indian context, to find the right language.

One of the most important and least publicized aspects of Gandhi's career during these years was his active participation in the cultural and political life of Gujarat.[3] He built a base there, and a network of relations which helped him in his political career. His involvement was not actuated by any deep 'identitarian' need. For Gandhi, his provincial sense of belonging was the result of a hazard of birth which did not carry deep significance. He was attached to the Gujarati language, yet he advocated the use of Hindi, or rather Hindustani, as the national language and displayed no provincial chauvinism. His search for a political base in Gujarat was pragmatic. To play a role in national politics, he needed a regional base and a group of friends.

Gandhi's entry into the political life of Gujarat happened to coincide with the political awakening in a province which had previously been little affected by nationalist agitations. It cannot be said that Gandhi was the catalyst of this awakening, but a certain conjunction occurred between his arrival and growing aspirations for change in a whole milieu of the urban middle class and the affluent peasantry. The emergence of Ahmedabad as the second centre of India's cotton textile industry after Bombay, and the attendant rise of a local industrial bourgeoisie sympathetic to nationalism, were important factors. Ahmedabad industrialists, in particular the enlightened Ambalal Sarabhai, gave Gandhi crucial financial support which helped him become a full-time political and social worker, without having to earn his living as a lawyer.

In 1917 Gandhi was elected President of the Gujarat Sabha, an old association created in 1885 mostly to deal with questions of local taxation. He used this as a vehicle to launch a campaign for constitutional reforms, in the course of which he forged useful links in the rural areas

---

[3] On this aspect, see J.M. Brown, *Gandhi's Rise to Power: Indian Politics 1915–1922*, Cambridge, 1972, pp. 92–111.

of the province. He was also chosen as head of a new association, the Gujarat Political Conference, which started a propaganda campaign in villages. He became actively involved in various associations which promoted the Gujarati language and Gujarati literature. He favoured the replacement of English with the vernacular as the language of teaching and communication. Gandhi's emergence as a national leader was underpinned by his capacity to mobilize the most active political elements in the province. Vallabhbhai Patel, whom he met in this period, was to become his most trusted political lieutenant. His political investment in Gujarat helped him acquire a position on the national scene, which South Africa alone had not been able to give him.

The defining moment was his encounter with the peasantry in Bihar. In the campaign he waged for the rights of indigo cultivators at Champaran, Gandhi not only discovered the true state of the Indian countryside, of which he was previously fairly ignorant, but more importantly he forged an image as a leader preoccupied with the poor. This allowed him, an outsider, to carve for himself a place at the centre of Indian political life. In Champaran he was able to refine the technique of satyagraha, adapting it to a context very different from South Africa. He learnt to operate on a much wider scale and to rely on a group of local activists whom he trained, and through whom he established contact with the peasantry.

In 1918, in Ahmedabad, he was closely involved in settling a labour dispute between the owners of cotton mills and their workers. His intervention helped the workers to gain some improvements without resulting in a defeat for the owners. During this strike, Gandhi first used fasting as a method. It was to become a central tool in his kit, to be used effectively in many different circumstances.

He still lacked a political idiom which would allow him to lead movements openly directed againtst colonial rule. This lacuna largely explains why his first intervention in national politics ended in a kind of fiasco. There remains an element of mystery as to the deep causes of his sudden irruption on the national political scene in 1919. Neither the *Autobiography*, nor the different biographies, give convincing explanations of Gandhi's decision to launch a campaign against the government. In the *Autobiography*, the narrative relating the launching of the Rowlatt satyagraha in March 1919 is strangely detached.

Gandhi recounts how he tried to persuade the viceroy, Lord Chelmsford, to drop the bill, and, faced with the latter's refusal, had no choice than to launch satyagraha. In a dream, he was given a hint that the best way to launch the movement was to call for a *hartal.* The country responded enthusiastically to the call. There was a dreamlike quality to the whole episode—as Erikson rightly noted. When Gandhi launched his appeal to satyagraha, it is clear he had no idea how it would be received. Hence the divine surprise at seeing the scale of the popular response. But at this point Gandhi could rely on no proper organization, and could therefore exercise no control over subsequent happenings. This explains why he was overcome with panic when things got out of hand, and why he had no choice but to stop the movement. In view of this first failed attempt, his capacity to keep control of the much wider non-cooperation movement of 1920–2 is truly astounding and has to be explained partly by the fact that he managed to make the Congress his instrument.

1920 saw an encounter between one man and a people; it was to have a deep and lasting impact on both. I shall come back later to the question of Gandhi's impact upon the Indian people. What about the impact of the people on Gandhi? How far was he transformed by the encounter?

The Transformation of Gandhi: Towards a New Political Idiom

The transformation in his external appearance, with the wearing of the *lungi* as a sign of solidarity with the poorest, has been mentioned, but a more important innovation was the adoption by Gandhi of a new political idiom which found an immediate resonance among the masses. He abandoned the struggle for any simple application in India of the norms which the British claimed to respect. He returned all his British medals and awards, making a clear breach with his past as a loyal albeit dissident subject of the Crown. In 1920 Gandhi clearly became an Indian nationalist and threw to the winds the imperial patriotism which had been part and parcel of his Indian patriotism. It is important to stress that his breach with the empire did not lead him to develop anti-British feelings. He continued to think that his struggle against British imperialism was also a struggle for the liberation of the British people. Although he came to view the imperial government

as 'satanic', he never extended the epithet to encompass its representatives, whom he always respected as individuals. He remained hopeful
till the end that he could convert the British to his point of view so as
to hasten the liberation of India and avoid violence.

The political objectives he defined in 1920, exemplified by the term
swaraj, had no connection with existence within the imperial framework. Gandhi did not invent the term, which was a literal translation
of 'Home Rule'—an idea popularized by the Irish struggle—always
a source of inspiration to Indian nationalism, but he gave it a new,
enlarged meaning. He was not bothered by the question whether
Swaraj meant dominion status or complete independence; that was a
problem for constitutional lawyers, and Gandhi had little interest in
that branch of the law. He wanted India to emancipate itself intellectually and spiritually not only politically. He was aware, as he had already
argued in *Hind Swaraj*, that political emancipation, unaccompanied
by spiritual emancipation, could be a sham. Emancipation had to start
at the economic level, and the crucial point seemed to him the generalized adoption of khadi. Swaraj and khadi were one and the same. By
1920 Gandhi had been able to find a political language in which he
could translate, in a form accessible to all, the aspirations of the Indian
people to political and economic emancipation.

There remained the 'social question', about which Gandhi was still
cautious. He had no independent source of income—he never became
a Congress functionary—and was therefore dependent on the generosity
of rich merchants and industrialists such as Ambalal Sarabhai, Jamnalal
Bajaj and Ghanshyamdas Birla. He had a frugal style of living, but, as
Sarojini Naidu once jokingly remarked, it cost his friends a great deal
of money to keep him in poverty. His consumption of fresh fruit, increasingly his staple diet, would have bankrupted many a middle-class
household. This friend of the poor was also a friend of the rich, and
he was always opposed to the ideology of class struggle. While he never
showed indulgence towards the rich, whom he expected to behave as
trustees and not owners of their assets, his links to business circles did
sometimes act as a brake on his political decisions.

Gandhi's advent to the leadership of the nationalist movement
cannot be accounted for either in determinist terms or as pure contingency. As early as 1909 he clearly manifested political ambitions,
directed towards India, and saw his struggle in South Africa within

that larger framework. The death of his mentor Gokhale just after Gandhi's return to India left him a kind of political orphan, and he had to fight to find his place in the nationalist movement, where, notwithstanding the reputation he had acquired in South Africa, nobody saw him as a messiah. He was able to play on his two major assets, the method of satyagraha and the idiom of Swaraj, to compete successfully with those who, after Tilak's death, appeared best placed to take over leadership of the movement, namely Motilal Nehru and C.R. Das. He was able to prevail upon them in 1920, largely because he could rely on a mass base, which the Khilafat movement offered him, but his work in Champaran and Gujarat also proved fruitful for it gave him the aura of a leader preoccupied with the poor. South Africa had allowed Gandhi to construct his personality as a public man and to acquire the basic competencies necessary for a political career. Now his leadership of India's nationalist movement was due to his capacity to exploit various opportunities offered by the Indian situation as it evolved in 1915–20, when he consolidated his base. Past the age of fifty, he had become the leader of a gigantic movement, of which there was no equivalent anywhere in the world. He told cheering crowds that India would soon get swaraj. It actually took almost thirty years for swaraj to come. Over these years, Gandhi often had a feeling of failure. To historians and the wider public, however, his name remains so indissolubly linked to India's eventual independence that his success, at almost every halting point, is taken almost always for granted.

CHAPTER 5

Gandhi and
Indian Independence

G andhi's contribution to the Indian freedom struggle was three-pronged: in the field of collective psychology, his intervention helped remove deep-seated Indian fears of the British and their power; in the realm of political organization, the reforms he accomplished transformed the Congress from a club of Anglicized lawyers into a mass political organization capable of widespread agitation; and in the development of mass agitation itself, Gandhi's role was essential in launching the three great campaigns of 1920–2, 1930–4, and 1942, weakening British rule and preparing the ground for independence.

Gandhi and the End of Fear

British colonial domination in India, in the manner of all such domination, was based on a combination of perpetrating violence and extracting consent. Although the conquest itself had come about as the result of a series of military campaigns, concluding in the violent putting down of the Great Rebellion of 1857, British rule did not rest only on military force. In the long term it was not possible for a few thousand Britishers to maintain a rule for two centuries over millions of Indians through sheer force. From the eighteenth century on, the British found powerful allies in India: princely rulers who calculated that alliance with the Company would allow them to get the better of rivals or pretenders, merchant groups that saw in the regime of Company Bahadur the source of substantial profits; and mercenaries attracted to the regular and relatively high pay offered by Company armies. The colonial administration and its armies always employed a majority of native personnel, mostly working in subaltern positions under the authority of Britishers, and these employees contributed in an essential way to the stability and durability of British rule. The only serious threat to the colonial regime came from the ranks of the native soldiery, when the sepoys rose in 1857.

The precise mechanisms through which the allegiance of these native collaborators, as well as the mass of colonial subjects, was ensured and perpetuated, changed over time. At the outset, Company Bahadur was perceived by many Indians as something of an 'indigenous' power which operated within the existing framework of local political culture. The Company's obstinacy in clinging to the fiction that it was a vassal of the Mughal emperor, even after the latter had become, after 1803, their puppet, earned it some measure of loyalty from the many who continued to see in the Mughal throne the fount of political legitimacy in India. After the abolition of the Mughal Empire in 1858 and the massacre of the imperial family in the wake of the Great Rebellion, there followed a dangerous vacuum in terms of legitimacy, which the British attempted to fill in 1877 by making Queen Victoria Empress of India. This succeeded in creating feelings of loyalty *vis-à-vis* the British sovereign in sections of the population, as is testified by the outpouring of homages in 1897, during the jubilee of the queen, but the loyalty was not only for love of the sovereign; it owed a lot to the presence in India, after 1858, of a massive British military force capable of preventing attempts at mutiny by native troops, and more generally to a racial inferiority complex among Indians carefully nurtured by the British.

There are well-known analyses of the psychology of colonized populations in the French colonial context by such authors as Albert Memmi and Frantz Fanon, and, *mutatis mutandis*, their insights can be usefully applied to the British Indian situation. In daily encounters with Britishers, which were becoming increasingly infrequent by the end of the nineteenth century, Indians were supposed to display recognition of their inferiority through carefully codified forms of behaviour. This created a charged atmosphere, well captured in works of fiction such as E.M. Forster's *A Passage to India*. For educated Indians most humiliating was the fact that, while some were ready to accord superiority to Western civilization over Indian traditional culture, they were expected to extend this recognition of superiority to every member of the ruling race, no matter how boorish he might be. This was a source of constant tension and often resulted in racial incidents. However, before the 1890s there were few Indians who dared defy these conventions and openly challenge the colonial masters in public. Gandhi himself, though raised in a princely state where the British presence was more lightly felt than in British India, imbibed from childhood a kind of respect mixed with fear *vis-à-vis* the colonial rulers. A popular ditty on the 'mighty Englishman'[1] made a strong impression on him:

> 'Behold the mighty Englishman
> He rules the Indian small,
> Because being a meat-eater
> He is five cubits tall'

Nehru, in an oft-quoted passage of his *Discovery of India*, expatiated on the atmosphere of fear in colonial India, 'fear of the army, the police, the widespread secret service; fear of the official class; fear of laws meant to suppress and of prison; fear of the landlord's agent; fear of the moneylender; fear of unemployment and starvation, which were always on the threshold'.[2]

For a few decades, individual acts of heroism appeared the only way to remove this fear. From the 1870s there were outbreaks of terrorist violence which recurred sporadically throughout the period of the freedom struggle. In the late nineteenth century, some extremist leaders of the Congress dared, for the first time, to enlarge the critique of the British from one aimed at the individual behaviour of Britishers to one directed at British pretensions to cultural superiority. Their anti-British discourse has been correctly analysed as being basically 'derivative', inasmuch as Indians turned their own ideal of masculinity against the British without criticizing it. They called on Hindus to recapture their pride through an internalization of these masculine values, the dominant values of Victorian Britain. British strictures against Indians, especially Hindus, as an 'effeminate' race (excluding the so-called 'martial races') struck a deep chord, and calls to Indian males to be more virile, via meat-eating and physical training, met with

---

[1] Quoted in *Autobiography*, op. cit., p. 18.
[2] J. Nehru, *The Discovery of India*, Delhi, 1994(1st edn, 1946), p. 358.

considerable success among vast sections of the urban population. In the late nineteenth century, even those Indians who rebelled openly against British rule were largely imbued with the values of the colonizers. For them the only possible way to fight colonial power was through a display of physical courage in direct military confrontations. The liberation of India, they thought, could come about only through the actions of a small élite group of heroes who had overcome their fear. The mass of the people, deemed too cowardly to rise, were supposed to remain passive and be content with supporting and applauding such heroes in their struggle.

Those Indians who did not adhere to such a 'masculine' concept of nationalism, but nevertheless resented being seen by the British as cowardly and effeminate, were seeking a formula which would help them recover their lost self-esteem. Gandhi's specific contribution was to offer a technique which allowed even those not trained in physcial combat to master their fear and act effectively. This was the technique of self-mastery, which belonged to the Indian tradition of yoga, but to which was added a collective twist. The satyagrahi's training aimed at helping him overcome his fear through control over his body. There were strong similarities with ascetic techniques, but for Gandhi asceticism was not the end; it was the means to an end. Ascetic techniques, particularly sexual continence aimed at the conservation of sexual energy, could be transformed into an active social force. Although Gandhi never demanded the individual satyagrahi's complete acceptance of his ideas on celibacy and vegetarianism, his emphasis on self-mastery implied the need to deploy these techniques.

Gandhi never sought to enrol a large number of participants in the exemplary actions he launched. Techniques of self-mastery cannot be easily acquired by a great number of people. He accomplished the Salt March with only seventy-nine companions. Gandhi's call to the masses to participate actively in political movements was always mediated through his small group of faithful followers who were meant to serve as examples to the masses. For the Mahatma, the majority of Indians were not meant to become satyagrahi; yet they were not expected to remain passive and be content to applaud the feats of the satyagrahi either. They were meant to be sufficiently inspired to launch their own non-violent actions, and court mass arrest. Gandhi used the state's weapon, imprisonment, very effectively as a political weapon against the state: he forced the British to arrest tens of thousands, causing a paralysis in the prison system. The experience of prison helped forge the character of the satyagrahi and sympathizers, allowing Gandhi to control them better.

In the struggles launched by Gandhi there gradually emerged a new type of individual, influenced by a value system different from the one common to the British and their terrorist/extremist adversaries—the system based on an exaltation of force as a manifestation of masculinity. Thanks to Gandhi, hundreds of thousands of 'ordinary' Indians belonging mostly to the middle classes could recapture their self-esteem without having to adopt a warrior's style of life and to turn to meat-eating (the two being closely linked in the popular perception). Gandhi helped them free themselves from a passive acceptance of the norms of behaviour imposed by the colonizer. There was a risk, of which Gandhi was aware, of bringing about the birth of a new élite, characterized not by aggressive physical courage, but by its capacity to endure sufferings of the flesh for the cause of the nation. Such an 'élite of suffering' did not crystallize in the same way as an 'élite of violence' might have.

Gandhi's position *vis-à-vis* masculinity was not, however, devoid of ambiguity. On the one hand he deplored the 'emasculation' of the Indian people brought about by the general confiscation of weapons which the British had effected, thus echoing one of the most widespread complaints voiced by nationalists in general against colonial rule. At the same time he was critical of the tendency to equate masculinity with the use of violence. He did not hesitate to praise femininity as a force different from brute force, despite his own fears of female sexuality. It was not on the basis of an appeal to 'masculine' values that he called on his countrymen to rid themselves of the fear they felt towards the British and which prevented them opposing even the most blatant injustices of colonial domination.

Gandhi's emancipatory project had a dual dimension: he first called on Indians to reject the 'syndrome of the victim'. He reminded them of the fact that their subjection to the British was not the result of fate but the outcome of their own actions. As he wrote in *Hind Swaraj*, the British did not conquer India, India gave itself to the conqueror and continued to do so. What had been given voluntarily could be taken back by a similar act of will. If Indians wanted to shake off British domination, they could; but they had first to reject the values which underpinned the colonial régime, above all the ideology of brute force. They had also to unite, and the method of satyagraha aimed at creating this unity. It allowed its adepts to mobilize their inner moral strength, to transform it, in the course of action, into a material force capable of overturning obstacles.

Observers noticed that there was a change in the attitude of Indians *vis-à-vis* the British around 1920. While there had previously been mostly fear and submission, albeit mixed with enormous resentment, a new attitude of quiet challenge became perceptible, to the oft-expressed exasperation of British rulers and administrators. Gandhi contributed to this change of atmosphere more by personal example than through his writings and speeches. In this respect, the emergence of a group of faithful disciples was very important, for it demonstrated that it was not necessary to be a Mahatma in order to be courageous and brave the lathis of the colonial police. These disciples served as intermediaries between Gandhi and the mass of the Indian people and they exemplified in the eyes of the latter the advent of a new type of individual capable of sacrificing himself for the cause of the nation without seeking personal reward. The call to sacrifice was an essential part of Gandhian teaching: it had deep resonances in both Hindu and Muslim culture (the notion of *shahid* or martyr), and it held a particular attraction for women. The fact that some of Gandhi's closest disciples were women had a considerable impact, and their example fired many Indian women with the courage to come out of the domestic space in which they had been traditionally confined, to appear in public for the first time.

There was an element of ambiguity in this Gandhian call to sacrifice addressed to women. While it gave them added importance and sowed a certain amount of confusion in the minds of the colonial authorities— the British were reluctant to use violence against women in the same way as against men—it also tended to reinforce traditional conceptions of women as wives and mothers sacrificing themselves for their men. But on the whole, given the context of colonial India, this call to sacrifice had undoubtedly an emancipatory dimension.

At the time of the Salt March in March–April 1930, the liberating aspect of Gandhi's teachings was demonstrated with particular clarity. Gandhi's decision to start the campaign of Civil Disobedience with a deliberate violation of the salt laws was at first understood neither by the British nor by many nationalists. It proved soon to be extraordinarily effective, for the salt tax was the only one all Indians, including the poorest, had to pay. It was a powerful symbol of the oppression of the Indian people by the colonial régime, and the popular response was overwhelming. The Salt March was a remarkable example of 'propaganda through deeds'. Once Gandhi himself had collected the salt, hundreds of thousands felt free to do the same and thus did not shirk from breaking colonial law. By doing this they freed themselves symbolically of their fear of colonial rule. The loss of prestige which the Raj underwent could never be repaired. Gandhi's ability to instil courage into the minds of ordinary people through the sheer force of his example comes out clearly from the well-known narrative by an English journalist of the repression of a demonstration before a salt depot in 1930:

> In complete silence the Gandhi men drew up and halted a hundred yards from the stockade. A picked column advanced from the crowd, waded the ditches and approached the barbed-wire stockade . . . Suddenly . . . at a word of command, scores of native policemen rushed upon the advancing marchers and rained blows on their heads with their steel-shod lathis. Not one of the marchers even raised an arm to fend off the blows. They went down like nine-pins. From where I stood I heard the sickening whack of the clubs on unprotected skulls. The waiting crowd of marchers groaned and sucked in their breath in sympathetic pain at every blow. Those struck down fell sprawling, unconscious or writhing with fractured skulls or broken shoulders . . . The survivors, without breaking ranks, silently and doggedly marched on until struck down . . . Although everyone knew . . . that within a few minutes he would be beaten down, perhaps killed, I could detect no signs of wavering or fear. They marched steadily, with heads up, without the encouragement of music or cheering or any possibility that they might escape serious injury or death. The police rushed out and methodically and mechanically beat down the second column. There was no fight, no struggle; the marchers simply walked forward till struck down.[3]

This almost unbearable narration produces an impression of malaise. It appears as a masochistic séance, when it was in fact very different. The capacity of the satyagrahi to resist physical suffering resulted from

[3] Quoted in L. Fischer, *Gandhi*, op. cit., pp. 298–9.

a training in which the ideology of self-sacrifice and restraint was a crucial component. In allowing themselves to be beaten almost to death (several demonstrators were killed that day), the satyagrahis were trying to break the will of the police. Even though, on that particular day, Indian policemen under the orders of British officers did not crack, it became obvious that the morale of the police could not survive months of confrontation of this kind.

There remain two unresolved questions: was Gandhian non-violence the only or even the main reason for the end of the fear felt by Indians *vis-à-vis* the British, and why had India to wait another twenty years to gain independence? It is difficult to give a definite answer to the first. Nehru eloquently put forward the thesis of Gandhi's essential contribution to the lifting of fear by equating his intervention with a psychoanalytical cure.[4] The loss of prestige of European colonial powers in Asia is, however, a complex phenomenon, and its roots go back to the defeat of Russia by Japan in 1905, which provoked a great swelling of pride in Asia, felt also in India, particularly in Bengal. It was enhanced by the First World War and the Russian Revolution, but the echo of these events was often muted in India outside the big cities. Gandhi's action tended to amplify an already existing trend: it affected social milieux, such as part of the middle classes (traders and merchants in particular) or middle peasants, who had remained unaffected by the surge of anti-imperialism provoked by these events. These social groups, which tended to be rather opportunistic in their political behaviour, were very sensitive to considerations of prestige: Gandhi helped them free themselves of their fear of the *sarkar* and many men and women belonging to this strata directly transferred their allegiance from the British sovereign to Gandhi. The appellation of 'uncrowned king of India' often attached to Gandhi after 1920 was not without meaning and such a transfer of allegiance had considerable political impact.

Regarding the second question, the existence of considerable internal differences in India must be borne in mind; Gandhi himself tended

[4] He wrote in *Discovery of India*, op. cit., p. 299: 'So, suddenly, as it were, that black pall of fear was lifted from the people's shoulders. . . . It was a psychological change, almost as if some expert in psychoanalytical method had probed deep into the patient's past, found out the origins of his complexes, exposed them to his view, and thus rid him of that burden.'

to underestimate them, and their manipulation by the British was an essential factor in allowing them to maintain their rule till 1947.

Gandhi as an Organizer

From the time of South Africa, Gandhi revealed considerable gifts as an organizer. He was very methodical, and in his campaigns paid much attention to the minutest detail. During the Salt March he kept close watch on the logistics of the operation, making sure that the participants were suitably fed, as the surviving notes testify. Gandhi was especially meticulous in his management of the funds entrusted him, and kept daily accounts. He proved at an early stage to be an extraordinarily effective fund-raiser, an activity to which he referred jokingly as 'milching the cow'. In the course of his long career Gandhi was involved in the creation of many organizations, most of them short-lived. The first was the Natal Indian Congress (although his exact role in its foundation is not clear), which was never a very effective organization, failing in particular to mobilize the mass of coolies which formed the bulk of the Indian population in South Africa. Later, in Transvaal, Gandhi created a specific organization to wage the satyagraha campaign, which did not outlast his departure from South Africa. His most decisive contribution remained the impetus he gave, after his return to India, to the transformation of the Indian National Congress into a mass organization.

The Congress was formed in 1885 as a club of gentlemen who met once a year to discuss India's problems and vote resolutions, which were then respectfully forwarded to and ignored by the colonial authorities. The first organizer of the Congress, Allan Octavian Hume, an Englishman, attempted unsuccessfully to endow it with a more or less permanent structure. In reality, till around 1920 Congress activities were largely limited to holding an annual session, a highpoint in the social and cultural as much as the political life of India. Most interventions in these sessions were delivered in the language of the colonizer—the only language all members of the élite were comfortable with, and one which presented also the advantage of being unconnected with a regional group. In the intervals between these sessions there was no sustained activity, except for the organization of occasional meetings and the publication of pamphlets with a limited circulation.

The movement had neither elected leaders nor fee-paying members nor a permanent secretariat (only a part-time general secretary) nor a press organ. Some of its members had been elected to the provincial councils after the Morley–Minto reforms of 1909 had introduced a certain amount of Indian representation in political institutions, but they were not elected on a party ticket: they got in as individuals. Prior to Gandhi's leadership the Congress was not equipped to launch mass agitation: it had neither the financial resources nor the personnel to engage in large-scale campaigns.

Gandhi acted as the catalyst for an in-depth reorganization of the nationalist movement. In 1920 he was specifically asked to reform Congress so as to make it a proper organization endowed with a permanent structure and capable of sustained activity. His major innovations were the institution of a fee calculated so as to be largely symbolic, allowing even members of low-income groups to join (but nevertheless excluding the really poor), and the formation of a pyramid of local and provincial committees which elected delegates to sit in a 'parliament' known as the All India Congress Committee. The latter elected a working committee which managed party affairs on a day-to-day basis. There was also a clause which required every member to spin a certain amount of khadi every day, but it was never strictly enforced, as it would have considerably reduced membership. Apart from these reforms Gandhi also managed to give the movement a sound financial basis through the launching of a national subscription for a Tilak Swaraj Fund, which raised substantial funds, mostly contributed by powerful Gujarati and Marwari business communities as well as by some princes. The success of the subscription was due in part to Gandhi's charisma and powers of persuasion, but also to the wave of enthusiasm generated by the non-cooperation movement.

The Congress, as it emerged from non-cooperation, was very different from the pre-war movement. It had several hundreds of thousands of fee-paying members, a grassroots organization in each district of British India (it did not cover the Indian states, for which the Indian States Peoples Conference was created in the 1930s), an elected all-India leadership, and generally the first modern political organization in the history of India. In the field of political organization, Gandhi was thus a modernizer who broke away from the élitist and clannish practices of his predecessors. The new Congress was not created *ex nihilo* by Gandhi; in his reformist attempt he had the full support of many leaders and cadres who wanted to make Congress an efficient political machine. It is probable that, but for his intervention, re-organization would have been a more gradual process and would have met with more determined opposition from some who had everything to lose from a democratization (however limited) of the movement.

Paradoxically, the next stage, that is the transformation of the Congress into a full-fledged political party, which became a party of governance at the provincial level from 1937, and at the national level in 1946, went against Gandhi's own ideas. The Mahatma had always expressed his preference for light, non-bureaucratic organizations, but he was powerless to prevent the gradual transformation of Congress into a bureaucratic machine. A crucial moment in the process was the formation of Congress governments in 1937 in seven of the twelve Indian provinces, under the reformed constitution granted by the British in 1935 at the end of the Civil Disobedience movement. Having to assume governmental responsibilities, the nationalist move-ment found itself forced to seek a compromise with the state bureau-cracy—which was in the process of being gradually Indianized—and there developed a certain ambiguity in the relationship between party and state which was to persist and increase after 1947. In spite of himself, Gandhi was not only the creator of a politico-bureaucratic machine which played a major role in India's accession to independence, he also contributed to keeping alive many traits of the colonial régime which he had wanted to abolish.

Gandhi's failure to prevent the bureaucratic normalization of the nationalist movement was partly due to the nature of his own political support base. From the 1930s Gandhi found himself increasing-ly identified with a dominant conservative faction of the Congress of which he became somewhat a prisoner. Most of his lieutenants, with the partial exception of Nehru, were men of the centre-right on the political spectrum, people who wanted a stabilization of the move-ment to prevent revolutionary troubles from disrupting the process of Indian independence. They saw in Gandhian non-violence an ideologically useful device to neutralize the left wing of the nationalist party, and they did not hesitate to make use of Gandhi for their own purposes. The Mahatma was not blind to their manoeuvres, but he let them act, partly because he had his own differences with the left, but also partly because the ideological hard core of his faithful followers was too small to allow him to impose his views on the Congress at large.

It is worth taking a quick look at the Gandhian milieu. It was actually a very heterogeneous assemblage of personalities with very different profiles and trajectories. There was the small group of ashram disciples, among whom the most remarkable were Mahadev Desai, the indefatigable private secretary, Gandhi's real *alter ego*, who followed him everywhere, even to jail; and Mirabehn, formerly Miss Slade, an English admiral's daughter who had been sent to Gandhi by Romain Rolland in 1922 and who was probably closer to him than anyone else. There was a second circle consisting of activists in various social movements, particularly the Harijan Seva Sangh; among them was Vinoba Bhave, whose role as Gandhi's spiritual heir has already been mentioned; and J.C. Kumarappa, secretary of the All India Spinners Association, concerned with the promotion of khadi. A third circle was composed of Congress leaders and activists close to the Mahatma but not totally dependent on him, as they generally had a political base of their own. They rallied to him largely because they saw that he alone could give Congress the popular base it lacked. The two most prominent in this circle were Vallabhbhai Patel and Jawaharlal Nehru. The former, a Gujarati lawyer, was probably the most faithful and effective of Gandhi's lieutenants. This pragmatic realist, capable of being very tough, was ideally suited to balance the Mahatma's sometimes woolly idealism, and after 1934 Gandhi increasingly relied on him for managing political affairs.

Gandhi's relationship with Nehru was more complex. Nehru was for him a sort of rebellious son. Educated at Harrow and Cambridge, Nehru was in many ways Gandhi's complete opposite: profoundly Anglicized, fascinated with industry and technology, he was influenced by Fabian socialism, and, in spite of his liberalism, attracted to the Soviet system as portrayed by the Webbs in their book *The Soviet Union: A New Civilization*. He had enormous affection and admiration for Gandhi and, despite their ideological differences, never dared openly confront the Mahatma. Gandhi used this close personal relationship to maintain a link with the younger generation of socialist-oriented Congressmen and keep them within the Congress fold.

Gandhi was largely instrumental in the emergence of this new political generation of men who were some twenty years younger than him, men who, while admiring him greatly, were socially more exposed to the influence of their environment. They were made up of a mixture of idealism and realism which made them effective leaders in independent India. Only two important nationalist leaders remained totally immune to Gandhi's influence: Jinnah, who evolved from a strict constitutionalist into the leader of the Muslim separatist movement; and Subhas Chandra Bose, a disciple of the Bengali leader C.R. Das (who died in 1925). Bose put forward a more aggressive interpretation of nationalism and, during the Second World War, sided with Japan in the hope of hastening India's independence. Jinnah was the only Indian politician whose popularity, limited to the Muslim quarter of the population, was even remotely comparable to Gandhi's, but there was complete contrast between the two men.

Gandhi's most durable political legacy in India was the creation of a great multi-class political party which was dominant till the early 1990s. From the late 1930s, that party ceased to represent truly Gandhian ideals, but Gandhi, who stopped his membership in 1934, never openly disavowed it, making it possible for his lieutenants to use his charisma to establish their own political legitimacy.

This kind of highly paradoxical success induces interrogations as to Gandhi's effective long-term political impact. One is confronted with the fact of the appropriation of Gandhi's ideas by certain social forces, a feature which I will discuss later. Let us take a closer look at the three major political campaigns of 1920–2, 1930–4 and 1942.

Gandhi's Role in Anti-British Campaigns, 1920–1942

Gandhi's first appearance on the all-India political scene with the 1919 Rowlatt satyagraha ended in a fiasco but made him known all over India. The non-cooperation campaign which he inspired and led between December 1920 and February 1922 was on a much bigger scale, the first significant challenge to British rule after 1858. The spark was provided by the opposition of many Indian Muslims to British policy towards the defeated Ottoman empire and their demand for preserving the Khilafat of Islam.

Gandhi became associated at an early stage with Muslim protests against British policy, a position which did not go down too well with many nationalists, wary of a movement they thought dominated by pan-Islamist elements. But it enabled Gandhi to use this apparently peripheral position to establish himself at the heart of the political debate. He forged an alliance with some Muslim leaders which helped him make his views prevail in Congress in spite of his lack of a proper base.

Gandhi's idea was to combine this movement, which was popular among Muslims, with the broad opposition to British policy which expressed itself over the Punjab events. The official Hunter report on the events of 1919 in Punjab was seen by most in India as a white-washing of Dyer's action at Amritsar and provoked widespread anger. In August 1920, in protest against the report, Gandhi sent back all his British decorations, medals and awards, in a strong symbolic gesture, and issued a call for non-cooperation with the government to last until the two wrongs of Khilafat and Jallianwallabagh had been redressed, and swaraj obtained. He then moved Congress to support his pro-gramme. Congress support was not easy to obtain, as most leaders were hesitant about the stand to take on Khilafat and voiced doubts as to the validity of the method of non-cooperation.

To push forward his programme Gandhi literally had to take power within the Congress, which he accomplished in two stages. At a special session of the Congress held in Calcutta in September 1920, Gandhi gained only a narrow victory in the Subjects Committee because of the opposition of influential leaders, but he had greater success in the open session. At the annual ordinary session held at Nagpur in December 1920 he obtained a much larger victory, thanks to C.R. Das, one of the most influential leaders, rallying to his cause. In Nagpur, the programme of non-cooperation was defined in detail. It included on the one hand mainly symbolic actions, such as the sending back of all British titles and decorations, and also more directly political ones, such as a boy-cott of councils and official courts. An important aspect was economic, with a call to boycott foreign cloth and adopt khadi. There was also a call for the withdrawal of pupils and students from official educational institutions and the creation of 'national' schools, where the curriculum would be turned towards the specific needs of India. The call for swaraj was undoubtedly the toughest step taken by Congress in the political field, even if swaraj remained vaguely defined; even bolder was the decision to adopt satyagraha as a method of struggle.

The movement met with undoubted, though unequal, success. In the earlier phase, emphasis was put mostly on the boycott of official schools and courts. Tens of thousands of pupils and students left official teaching institutions and enrolled themselves in hundreds of 'national' schools created in a great surge of enthusiasm. Two hundred lawyers resigned from the bar and the number of court cases dropped significantly. On the other hand, only a few people sent back their titles and decorations which showed that loyalism towards the Crown remained deeply entrenched within the élite. In a later phase the greatest efforts were directed to the national subscription (Tilak Swaraj Fund) and to the mass enrolment of new members in Congress (hundreds of thousands joined). In the summer of 1921, with Gandhi's direct intervention, the boycott of foreign cloth intensified and great heaps of cloth were publicly burned all over India in what appeared to be rituals of cleansing by fire, which raised doubts in the minds of two close friends of Gandhi's, C.F. Andrews and Rabindranath Tagore, who detected in all this a streak of nihilism. But the movement went on with very little violence, and with the participation of large crowds in which Muslims and Hindus mingled in a demonstration of communal harmony, a sight unprecedented in India. The strength of the movement was demonstrated in spectacular fashion at the time of the visit to India of the heir to the throne, the Prince of Wales (the future Edward VII), when a hartal was massively observed across the country and the royal visitor had to make his way through deserted streets. In Bombay, however, things got out of hand as police and demonstrators fought pitched battles while there were attacks on British civilians. Gandhi was indignant at this first outburst of violence and condemned it in the strongest terms. At the beginning of 1922 the viceroy, Lord Reading, shaken by the width and breadth of the movement, was considering political concessions, when, on 11 February following the death of twenty-two policemen at the hands of an enraged crowd in Chauri-Chaura, a village in UP, Gandhi, without consulting anyone, and on the prompting of his 'inner voice', suddenly called off the movement.

While the colonial authorities, increasingly worried at the impact of the agitation, welcomed his move with a sigh of relief, even though they were doubtful of its effectiveness, in the nationalist camp there was sheer stupefaction, often laced with suppressed anger. And yet, as if by magic, the movement suddenly stopped in its tracks—this was an amazing demonstration of the moral authority which had by now been gained by Gandhi. To the end of his life, the Mahatma continued to defend his decision to call off the movement. He said the masses had not really understood his message of non-violence, and that he was forced to stop the movement lest he be held responsible for further violence. There are actually many indications that, for Gandhi, Chauri-Chaura was only the immediate pretext; for many weeks he had been disturbed by the rise of violence and become convinced that it was necessary to call for a pause.

His sudden decision to stop the movement while it was still in force has drawn criticism from historians, some of whom blame Gandhi for having broken the dynamics of the nationalist movement; but later developments prove them wrong. The movement started again after a few years with increased force, with a rejuvenated and strengthened Congress. From Gandhi's point of view, however, the crucial question was the possibility of violence. It showed that he had not been able to find a formula for mobilizing masses without incurring the risk of murderous outbursts. In the years to come he was to try to refine his methods without ever being able to completely achieve his objective.

In spite of its failure to significantly influence British policy towards the Khilafat (in fact it was Mustapha Kemal who suppressed it), the balance sheet of non-cooperation was on the positive side. It played a decisive role in accelerating the transformation of the Indian nationalist movement into a mass phenomenon and it inflicted on the Raj a loss of prestige from which it never really recovered. It also helped Gandhi, who was jailed, to acquire the aura of martyrdom, reinforcing his prestige as a leader.

But it also revealed fragility in the Gandhian leadership. Gandhi has generally been seen, and rightly so, as a charismatic leader whose success owed more to the type of personalized relationship established with his followers than to control of a political apparatus. However, to speak in Weberian terms, for such a leadership to become durable a certain degree of 'routinization of charisma' must take place.

Gandhi's particular kind of charisma did not lend itself to routinization, and partial withdrawal from political life appeared an appropriate solution. In 1920–2 Gandhi did not acquire a permanent grip on the Congress, but the moral authority he had gained made him the ultimate arbiter in case of difficulties. Six years after Chauri-Chaura, the leaders who had taken over the Congress had no choice but to call on him once again.

In the intervening years, between the end of non-cooperation and the launching of Civil Disobedience, Gandhi worked assiduously to enlarge his political base, in particular in merchant circles, and his efforts in fighting untouchability and promoting khadi benefited from the financial support given him by prominent businessmen. The same years also saw a parting of ways between Gandhi and some of the Muslim leaders of the Khilafat, which, in the long term, proved detrimental to Gandhi's leadership. From 1926 onwards there occurred a clear degradation in communal relations, as witnessed by the regular occurrence of riots. As a result, when Gandhi launched Civil Disobedience in 1930, the response from Muslims was muted, except in the Northwest Frontier Province, where the charismatic leadership of Abdul Ghaffar Khan mobilized local Pathans on a large scale.

Leaving aside the question of Muslim participation, Civil Disobedience revealed a deepening of the influence of Gandhi and his methods over the nationalist movement. First the movement defined as its ultimate objective the gaining of complete independence (*Purna Swaraj*) rather than dominion status, a point on which there was convergence between Gandhi's views and those of the more radical elements in Congress, such as Jawaharlal Nehru. But the ascendancy of Gandhi was visible mostly in the way in which he was able to conduct the movement, effectively from start to finish. When, at the end of 1929, the viceroy failed to answer positively the demand for a complete overhaul of the constitution put forward by the Congress one year earlier, a decision was taken to start a movement of civil disobedience. Full powers were given to Gandhi to decide the pace and exact shape of this movement. The Mahatma hesitated for a few weeks, and then his 'inner voice' gave him the solution. In a letter sent to the viceroy, Lord Irwin, in March 1930—very representative of Gandhi's political style—he put forward eleven points, all pertaining to economic and social problems faced by the Indian population at a time when the

Depression had started hurting them. Gandhi chose to focus more specifically on the question of the salt tax, whose abolition he demanded. This shows great pragmatism, a deep sense of the realities of the situation, as well as the extraordinary authority he had acquired— for the abolition of the salt tax was only a relatively minor point in the Congress programme.

An analysis of the Civil Disobedience movement gives a clear insight into the strengths and weaknesses of the Gandhian leadership. Gandhi's strongest point was his capacity to innovate, to catch his opponent by surprise and convince public opinion of the validity of his decisions. It can be said that Gandhi was greater as a tactician than as a strategist, for he never assured his retreat or prepared a position of withdrawal. But he knew how to exploit all the possibilities offered by a given situation, combining agitation and propaganda in a most effective way. Gandhi proved to be a genius of 'agitprop'; he was good at attracting the attention of the media upon his actions and on the movements he led. The start of the Salt March was covered by the three film documentary organizations present in India and by correspondents of the international press. Gandhi was skilled at staging his smallest action, so as to maximize its resonance, by playing on symbols and visual elements. When he seized the initiative, he gave no breathing time to the opponent, forcing the British to react in an *ad hoc* fashion, without quite managing to guess the Mahatma's next move. The British could never decide whether it was better to have him safely in jail or let him roam free. They always took their time before arresting him, which left him time to put things in place and let these then develop their own dynamic.

A close look at the Salt March allows us to understand Gandhi's conception of 'staging'. At the beginning of 1930 he created a cloud of mystery around his intentions. To Rabindranath Tagore, who came to visit him in his ashram, he said he was in the dark and did not know what he would do. Then he sent Irwin the eleven-point letter, which was supposed to remain secret to leave the viceroy time to answer. But the latter came out in the press, following a leak (the source is not known, but it does not appear to have been Gandhi himself). As the viceroy, taken by surprise, hesitated over his answer, Gandhi suddenly announced he would focus exclusively on the question of salt and the abolition of the salt tax. The British thought this a hoax and failed to understand the appeal of the issue. Gandhi then conceived the idea of the Salt March, and there was expectation in the air; the whole country came to a halt as Gandhi marched.

Thanks to the press and the newsreels, whose contents were disseminated orally throughout the entire countryside, the mass of the population appears to have followed Gandhi and his companions step by step as they marched through Gujarat from Ahmedabad to Dandi. The movement attracted attention abroad as well, and the American press gave it significant coverage. Gandhi took advantage of the march to organize meetings in all the places he passed through. At the end of the march, attention moved from Gandhi towards the many actions launched in the country to collect salt in breach of the government monopoly. Initially the authorities remained fairly passive, adopting the typical British attitude of 'wait and see', but this passivity, which was seen as weakness, favoured the quick spread of the movement. When the authorities decided to strike, one of their first moves was to arrest Gandhi. But far from acting as a brake on the movement, this gave it further élan, as Congress activists and sympathizers threw themselves into the battle. Eventually Gandhi's action resulted in a near-paralysis of the administration, hit by the resignation of many lower-grade employees not able to bear the public ostracism they suffered by being associated with an increasingly unpopular government.

An agitation which had started over a relatively minor but highly symbolic issue came to threaten law and order, and the viceroy had to accept direct negotiation with Gandhi, as well as make concessions to him. Apart from the issue of salt, the boycott of foreign cloth was highly successful, as pickets lined in front of the cloth shops and many merchants stopped dealing in foreign cloth. Imports of British cloth dropped considerably and this worried the Lancashire millowners, for whom India was a crucial market.

But a closer analysis reveals certain limitations in Gandhi's leadership. Even if the movement remained on the whole non-violent, there were episodes of violence. There were riots in Sholapur, the industrial city in Maharashtra, and there was a real popular rising in Peshawar, where a platoon of native troops refused to open fire on demonstrators and had to be replaced by Gurkhas—whose intervention resulted in severe loss of life. Terrorist elements also made use of the atmosphere of unrest to launch daring attacks, such as the Chittagong armoury raid, which resulted in an open battle between revolutionaries and the police, while in Delhi Bhagat Singh and his friends threw a bomb into the Central Legislative Assembly (it did not explode), an outrage for which they were sentenced to death and hanged amidst popular protest.

Gandhi, while he deplored their act, refused to condemn them and joined in the protests against their execution. The threat of violence remained, and the worries it created among moderate nationalist circles, and even more among traders and industrialists, was one of the factors which led Gandhi to seek a compromise with the viceroy. It was actually difficult to maintain control over a movement of such magnitude and, the longer it lasted, the more likely it was to result in outbursts of violence.

In order to ensure that the movements he led did not peter out, it was thus imperative that Gandhi obtain results in a relatively short span. After a whole year of agitation which had not resulted in any significant concession from London, Gandhi was led to accept a compromise—as epitomized by the so-called Gandhi–Irwin Pact of 1931—which suspended Civil Disobedience in exchange for minor British concessions. Gandhi even accepted to attend the second round of the Round Table Conference held in London while he knew that, in the face of the opposition of princes and other elements co-opted by the British, he had no chance of making his point of view and that of Congress prevail. There was an implied admission in this that his method had limitations. When the conference ended in deadlock, Gandhi had no choice but to go back to India and launch Civil Disobedience anew in much more unfavourable conditions. This time the British were not caught unawares and had no great problem curbing the movement, which dragged on without significant results throughout 1932 and 1933, amidst massive and often brutal repression, until it gradually faded away.

Civil Disobedience was undoubtedly Gandhi's finest hour, and never afterwards did he obtain such a level of popular mobilization around objectives he had himself defined, with the methods he had taught. The last large-scale movement in which he was involved, Quit

India, represented a different case. It was launched at a time when the Japanese were at the borders of India, having overrun Burma, and, although they had neither the intention nor the means to attack India (a fact of which Gandhi was probably not aware), it rested on a miscalculation about the determination of the British. Gandhi did not play an active role in the movement: he was arrested at its outset. The agitation gave a good pretext to 'hardliners' in the colonial government to try and crush Congress once and for all. They failed to achieve that end, but the outbreak of violence on a large scale did tarnish the image of Congress in the eyes of the Western public. More importantly, the disappearance of Congress from the official political scene, and its turn to underground activity, helped its rivals, namely the Muslim League and the Communist Party, strengthen their organizations and political influence. In the long term, however, the Quit India movement hastened the march towards Indian independence by showing the British that it was useless to try to remain in India by force in the face of determined opposition on the part of the Indian people. More decisive probably was the INA (Indian National Army) episode. The treason of native troops was seen by the British as an ominous portent of things to come if they attempted to remain in India by force.

Gandhi was not very directly involved in the events of 1944–7 which led to the actual independence of India, but the cumulative effect of the three great campaigns he had launched was to decisively weaken the will of the British to stay in India. Gandhi's role was also important in maintaining the unity of the nationalist movement when it faced growing ideological divisions after 1934. In 1920 he effected a sort of synthesis between the views of pre-war extremists and moderates. While himself a close disciple of Gokhale, he had defined a method of mass agitation which appealed to some of the extremists, with the exception of the terrorist fringe. The opposition which appeared in the Congress in 1923 between no-changers, faithful to Gandhian methods, and Swarajists, favourable to council entry, was basically a tactical divergence without ideological foundation. It was resolved in 1928 when Congress opted anew to boycott the councils.

From 1934, following the abandonment of Civil Disobedience, real ideological divisions appeared which pitted a moderate majority claiming inspiration from Gandhi against a leftist minority regrouped around the Congress Socialist Party, which in its turn was infiltrated by Communists following the new instructions of the Komintern after 1935. Gandhi was clearly on the side of the moderates, but he took care not to put the Left into a kind of ghetto, and to include some of its representatives in the Congress leadership. He was largely instrumental in having Nehru elected Congress President at the Lucknow Congress session in April 1936. Nehru had to work with a working committee dominated by moderates and was forced to accept the formation of Congress provincial governments in 1937, a move the Left was completely opposed to. By co-opting Nehru in this fashion, Gandhi succeeded in weakening the Congress left, which never represented a threat to the majority afterwards. When in 1939 Subhas Bose, having been elected President of Congress, tried to re-create a Left coalition to confront the moderates, Gandhi intervened directly to have him defeated and Bose was forced to resign.

Bose's departure resulted in a minor schism within Congress. It was the last open intervention by Gandhi in the internal power politics of Congress (of which he was not officially a member since 1934). The preservation of the unity of the Congress, in spite of the rise of a leftist wing within the party, helped it survive the period of underground activity of 1942–4 and facilitated its re-emergence in 1945–6 as a dominant political force. In the latter phase, the essential role was played by Gandhi's two main lieutenants, Patel and Nehru. It was one of the most brilliant moves of the Mahatma to have chosen as his de facto successors these two men who, in spite of an opposition in ideas and temper, could work as a team and complement each other.

Gandhi's profile as a political leader was certainly most original and totally different from that of all the other great political leaders of the century. A charismatic leader who established an almost physical relationship with his people, Gandhi never sought to institutionalize his political position.

Does this mean that he refused power? He certainly preferred influence to power, as shown by his trajectory after 1934, when he renounced any open political role, and did not renew his Congress membership. But he kept an eye on developments in the nationalist movement, and did not hesitate to intervene behind the scenes. His ability to keep overall control of Congress at least till 1942 shows he was no saint who had meandered into politics, but a consummate politician perfectly aware of the balance of forces and determined to make his views prevail in the face of opposition. His attitude towards state power remained complex. Despite views sometimes bordering on anarchism, he seems to have been aware of the importance of the state and to have seen it as a limited but effective agency for social change, as demonstrated in his support of prohibition.

His creative contribution to Indian political life, in the field of organization as well as political vocabulary, was considerable. He invented or popularized most of the terms that form the basic political vocabulary of India, in this sense he was without doubt one of the greatest political lexicographers of the twentieth century. And yet his political career ended on a major failure, the partition of India. What was his role in that tragedy?

Gandhi was not a communal or even a communitarian leader. His brand of religiosity left no place for communitarianism: his was a very personal religion which belonged to the Hindu fold only in a very general sense. Hinduism, however, is not a dogmatic faith, and a loose adherence to the faith, via bhakti, is widespread. Although his religion was not communitarian, Gandhi had some sense of the existence of a Hindu community: there is no clearer proof of it than his obstinate fight against the granting of separate electorates to Untouchables, while he accepted this for Muslims. Yet his nationalism was inclusive rather than exclusive: in contrast with Hindu nationalists, he accepted Indian Muslims (as well as Parsis, Jews and Christians) as constitutive parts of the nation as much as Hindus. But it must be accepted that his mental universe and the idiom he used had a clear Hindu connotation (with some Christian notions thrown in) and could therefore shock Muslim sensitivities. He was not from a region where a deep cultural synthesis had occurred between Islam and Hinduism—of the kind which had taken place in northern India, and his knowledge of Muslim religion and culture was limited. When he addressed Muslims, they did not feel he was one of them; he had a much more natural rapport with Hindu crowds.

He became increasingly alienated from the Muslim political leadership as it reorganized itself in the 1930s, around the Muslim League. He had a particularly difficult relationship with Jinnah. As a result, there was a growing gap between him and the Muslim masses. Although he fought determinedly against the project of Partition and took enormous personal risks at the end of his life to protect Muslims in India from attacks, he was not able to conduct a fruitful political dialogue with the leadership of the Muslim League, and it was left to Patel and Nehru, both very hostile to Muslim separatism, to conduct the final negotiations leading to Partition. Insufficient knowledge of and empathy for Indian Islam were probably at the root of Gandhi's difficulty in defining an appropriate response to the rise of Muslim nationalism.

Beyond his activity as an organizer and a political leader, Gandhi sought above all to reform Indian society so that independence could mean a real change and not a simple reshuffling of the instruments of rule.

CHAPTER 6

Gandhi and Indian Society
The Reformer and His Legacy

From the time of his return to India in 1915, Gandhi combined political activity with social reform. As early as *Hind Swaraj*, he had argued that independence, if it was not accompanied by a deep change in social priorities, would be pointless. Social reform meant primarily the eradication of poverty in the countryside through a reworking of social values and norms. For this objective, coordinated changes had to take place in several domains at the same time. The first step was to rehabilitate manual labour, traditionally despised by the upper castes. This was to lead to the rebirth of village industries, which alone would allow seasonal unemployment and rural poverty to reduce. This reorientation of socio-economic priorities had to be combined with the abolition of untouchability. Society as imagined by Gandhi would be neither 'modern' nor 'traditional' but would end the exploitation of the masses. It is necessary to keep in mind that Gandhi was not trying to put forward some utopia; he wanted to proceed gradually on the basis of existing realities. He divided his proposals between a 'minimal programme' which could be put into effect immediately, and a 'maximal programme' for which he fixed no time-frame. It is not, however, easy to differentiate between the two levels.

Gandhi and the Dignity of Manual Labour

In the dominant brahminical culture of India, manual labour is linked to the castes which occupy the lowest position. The idea of the dignity of manual labour was borrowed by Gandhi from Ruskin and Tolstoi.

The notion of 'bread labour', used by Tolstoi, was, according to Gandhi, one he had himself borrowed from another Russian author,

Bondarev. In this view, everyone has to earn his bread with the sweat of his brow; those who are not blessed being born peasants and artisans must find substitute activities to avoid idleness. The reason why this notion exercised a strong pull on Gandhi from the time of his South African stay may be partly to do with an aesthetic ideal. Although Gandhi does not appear to have been very influenced by considerations of aesthetics, they were not unimportant for him either. He had developed an appreciation for the craftsmanship of the artisan, and one of the most damning characteristics of modern civilization, in his eyes, was the ugliness it produced on a massive and unprecedented scale. He extended his aesthetic ideal to all forms of labour, including the humblest and most demeaning. It is clear that, for him, manual labour possessed a sacred essence and constituted a privileged way of reaching the divine. Gandhi was not inclined towards mysticism and did not give meditation much role as a technique towards the divine. It was through the most humble physical tasks that he found himself in communion with Creation and the Creator. This 'pragmatic' aspect of his religiosity can be seen as a legacy of his merchant caste origins. For Hindu merchants, the fulfilling of humble material tasks is one of the paths to divine knowledge.

Gandhi first tried to put into effect this idea in South Africa at the micro-social level of the communities he formed in the Phoenix and Tolstoi farms, and, after his return to India he attempted to give it a macro dimension. He seems to have thought that it was possible to move easily from one level to the other, that what could be done in his ashram could be replicated on an all-India scale. There is probably here the reflection of a Hindu cosmology, in which microcosm and macrocosm are two closely linked and interchangeable realities.

An inquiry into Gandhi's notion of society in general, and more particularly of Indian society, leads to the conclusion that it remained very imprecise and untheorized. There was no Gandhian sociology, even in an embryonic state: he does not even appear to have considered sociology a legitimate discipline. One does not find in his writings any attempt at sociological analysis, beyond a broadly drawn contrast between the mass of the poor and a small minority of the rich. He carried methodological individualism very far, to the point that he did not recognize the existence of social groups. In his view, society was a collection of individuals whose links were mostly of a territorial nature: village, province, nation were the only relevant groupings for him, much more than caste and class. He was unabashedly in favour of 'uniformization' because for him the real differences between individuals were internal. Thus he wished all Indians, whatever their provincial origin and their social or religious affiliation, to wear the same white khadi to symbolize the unity of the nation in the face of British oppression. In his view such uniformity did not threaten the individuality of each human being, which manifested itself in the specific relationship each individual soul had with God. In the same way, he wished everyone to fulfil the same tasks so as to erase social differences—which he did not, however, seek to abolish.

To publicize the idea of the dignity of manual labour, so foreign to the dominant ethos, he relied primarily on the exemplary value of his ashram, which he viewed as a kind of laboratory for social experiments, susceptible to being generalized. Yet in spite of Gandhi's discourse on self-sufficiency, the ashram never lived on its own resources: without Ambalal Sarabhai's generous initial donation and Ambalal's sister's continuous financial support, Gandhi would have had to close it down. The principles Gandhi tried to apply in it were, first that everyone had to perform manual tasks so as to undermine the traditional division of labour; and second that there were no ignoble tasks, and that, in particular the cleaning of latrines—traditionally reserved for Untouchables because deemed polluting—was actually ennobling. On this second point, he met with resistance even in his own family and entourage. In South Africa he had had a fight with his wife over it. How can one account for Gandhi's obsessive focus on the cleaning of toilets? Its origins must be found in a mixture of Victorian hygienist ideas about microbial transmission and his desire to fight traditional conceptions of purity and impurity, in which Gandhi saw a perversion of Hindu ideals. In this field, Gandhi was undoubtedly a modernizer and an enemy of tradition.

In preaching thus Gandhi targeted both the division of labour in traditional society and the parcellization of tasks typical of modern industrial society. The intellectual foundations of his position are to be found in a very specific combination of anti-authoritarianism and anti-intellectualism. Gandhi's anti-authoritarian position was rooted in the idea that command and control tasks were not intrinsically superior to execution tasks, and did not justify a higher social status for those who managed rather than worked. His anti-intellectualism was manifest in the fact that he did not recognize the specificity of intellectual labour and did not find acceptable the existence of a category of intellectual workers exempt from manual work. Although this points towards egalitarianism, his position was not devoid of ambiguity. For the greater part of his life he was reluctant to give up the social hierarchy of *varna*, even if he pleaded for a different way of sharing tasks. (In particular he thought Brahmins had to clean latrines, a view few of them shared.) Towards the end of his life, even though he became more critical of the varna hierachy, he did not completely repudiate it. He did not advocate any forced equality in income, either through the widespread redistribution of property or through taxation. He accepted that capitalists could have high incomes provided they effected a redistribution through the financing of welfare and social reform activities. He was not dismissive of merchant activity as such and recognized the importance of financial and accounting expertise.

Basically his conception was non-utilitarian, and he saw work as an essential moral value. His attitude towards the creation of wealth was ambivalent: he did not reject wealth per se but saw accumulation as an anti-natural process. He was in favour of the prudent management of public funds and criticized waste in the name of a traditional merchant ethic, which was different from the spirit of modern capitalism. He was not opposed a priori to technological innovation but did not accept the spiral of perpetual aggrandizement which defines modernity. Although not opposed to leisure and entertainment (though he himself had little time for them)—provided they did not take up too much time—he saw idleness as the 'mother of all vices', and the seasonal unemployment affecting all Indian peasants during part of the year as the greatest threat to the moral fibre of the nation. This was one of his major arguments in favour of reviving village industries, the ruination of which he viewed as one of the most disastrous outcomes of British rule.

Another source of his programme of reconstruction was a rather strange-sounding 'theory of proximity'. He mixed in an unusual fashion economic nationalism with localism. On the one hand, he was much influenced by the kind of 'neomercantilist' school of economic nationalists represented by Dadabhai Naoroji and M.G. Ranade— who had denounced the economic exploitation of India through a drain of wealth and the deindustrialization fostered by the forced opening of the Indian market to British goods,[1] particularly textiles. On the other hand, he defended a policy of limiting exchange within the country and favouring self-sufficiency at the village level, in parti- cular in the matter of textiles. He explained his views in relation to a notion of solidarity: for him it was mandatory to get supplies from neighbours rather than faraway suppliers, even if they were Indian. He berated the inhabitants of his native province, Saurashtra, for getting their supply of construction materials from elsewhere in India when materials were at hand in their own province. He did not conceive of independent India as a unified national market within which goods circulated freely on a large scale, because he saw such a model skewed in favour of big cities, to the detriment of villages. His ideal was rather a collection of largely autonomous micro-regional units with minimized exchange between them. Despite views to the contrary, he was not a spokesman for a 'national bourgeoisie' seeking to create a national market behind high protective barriers. His programme for village reconstruction sought other aims.

Gandhi and the Reconstruction of the Indian Village

Gandhi's 'constructive programme', which became his major pre- occupation after 1924 and focused most of his attention when he was not involved in his great political campaigns, was centred around the village. He was convinced that the real India was the 500,000 villages where, according to the 1921 census, 90 per cent of all Indians lived. He saw cities as artificial structures feeding on the countryside and

[1] See B. Chandra, *The Rise and Growth of Economic Nationalism in India. Economic Policies of Indian National Leadership 1880–1905*, Delhi, 1966.

acting as a relay for the foreign influence he wanted to extirpate in order to give India back its dignity. In his vision for the future of India, cities had only a minor role. He seemed to have thought that if his programmes for the economic reconstruction of villages were implemented, the cities would gradually fade away because they would lose their essentially parasitical functions. Gandhi's critique of the city seemed to be born of the fusion between Ruskin and Tolstoi's general denunciation of it as the locus of satanic modernity, and the more narrowly focused critique by economic nationalists of the Indian city as the lynchpin of the imperialist exploitation of India. The only kind of urban agglomeration which escaped these strictures was the small town living in close interaction with its rural environment; great metropolises, on the other hand, were for him monstrous outgrowths. Perhaps this contrast had its roots in his personal history, in the shock represented by the move to Bombay and London after a childhood spent in Porbandar and Rajkot.

His conception of the village was based on the one hand on his reading of a large corpus of orientalist and nationalist literature, tending to idealize the old Indian village community as a place of social harmony and non-exploitative economic exchange, and on the other hand on 'fieldwork' done during numerous tours of the countryside, carried out after 1915. The villages he saw during these tours came to symbolize for him the economic, social and moral degradation of India under colonial rule. He was particularly repelled by the lack of hygiene and sanitation, but also by the massive seasonal unemployment which kept the male population in the throes of idleness and attendant vices, in particular alcoholism. The contrast between an idyllic vision of the pre-colonial village (as drawn by many authors) with its artisans milling about and the clink of spinning wheels, and contemporary reality as he had seen it, appeared the strongest indictment of the evils of imperialism. His vision of the village was thus partly shaped by the credence he gave an idealized image. Although he probably did not entirely believe in the myth, it suited him not to abandon it for it helped to make his programme of reconstruction appear less utopian. His focus on seasonal unemployment, however, was truly insightful, for the problem, although familiar to social workers, had been generally ignored by economists and policy-makers.

As regards the solutions he offered, they are to be found scattered among many writings, often of a contradictory nature.[2] The broad outlines of his programme of socio-economic reconstruction were however clearly defined. The central point was the rebirth of village industries. As far as the purely agricultural aspect was concerned, Gandhi did not study the agrarian question in great depth and was often content with mouthing platitudes about the need for zamindars to behave humanely towards tenants. He appeared not to have been too bothered about the unequal distribution of land, thinking that the abolition of land revenue would give even the poorest peasants sufficient leeway to solve the problem of poverty without massive redistribution. On this point he was not very realistic, because by the third decade of the twentieth century land revenue was far from being the burden it had been for the peasantry a few decades earlier. Massive indebtedness was the greatest problem confronting most Indian agricultural producers. Gandhi did not take a clear position on the question: he had to be careful not to antagonize the powerful merchant communities, such as the Marwaris, who held a good part of the peasant debt and opposed the adoption of measures to reduce it. Gandhi apparently thought that the problem could be solved if only peasants found other sources of income, outside agriculture.

It was not via agricultural development that he saw the salvation of the Indian village. Towards the end of his life he paid more attention to the technical problems of improvement in cultivation, but did not give them central place in his scheme of things. He did not give much thought either to the problem of investment in agriculture. He took it for granted that the development of credit cooperatives would allow the financing of agriculture without aggravating peasant indebtedness. For him the major problem lay in the exclusive reliance of villagers on agricultural production, which forced them to buy goods outside the village, in particular cloth, which accounted for the largest non-food outlay in rural budgets. This was the crux of the matter, because the structure of exchange was skewed to the detriment of agricultural producers who had to pay high prices for cloth while the prices of their crops kept going down. From 1926 onwards, prices of agricultural

[2] For a selection of texts, see M.K. Gandhi, *Village Swaraj*, Ahmedabad, 1962.

products were on a downward spiral, which was accelerated with the onset of the Great Depression of the 1930s.

To remedy this structure of unequal exchange, the only way was for agriculturists to produce their own cloth, as Gandhi thought they had done in the past (while in fact only some villages specialized in cloth production and others were supplied from outside). In Gandhi's view, a resurgence of cotton spinning and weaving in villages (the latter had survived in some parts of India, particularly the south, where it had even experienced a kind of renaissance, but the former had totally disappeared), making use of locally available raw material, had also the advantage of solving the problem of seasonal unemployment among agriculturists. During the slack agricultural season they would busy themselves spinning and weaving cotton, which would allow them to be self-sufficient in cloth and result in a fall in unproductive expenses (especially on festivals and drink). It must be noted that, in spite of the emphasis laid on the voluntary character of reforms, Gandhi did not shirk from the use of coercive methods when advocating the prohibition of alcohol.

Gandhi also argued in favour of developing in villages various other industries for transforming agricultural products or, for instance, manufacturing utensils. Gandhi's programme was a combination of two different aspects: first, a plea for industrial decentralization, which was not unique to him or particularly utopian, even if its actual implementation posed a series of problems that he had not sufficiently thought through; second, an attempt to demechanize textile production through a return to the *charkha* (the traditional spinning wheel), which was clearly utopian and unfeasible because it did not take into account the question of cost. Artisanal cloth produced from non-industrial thread could have been viable only if it had been protected by a system of internal custom duties or if the cost of labour had been so compressed as to be close to zero.

In his lifetime, Gandhi was able to define only the broad outline of a programme and to inspire some initiatives aimed at the rehabilitation of village industries. His success here was unequal. The Congress governments formed in 1937 in most Indian provinces tried, during the two-year period when they were in power, to put into effect some points of the Gandhian programme. Some, particularly the Madras government, imposed the prohibition of alcohol and took measures to help village industries. Gandhi's advocacy of prohibition was based on ethical considerations, and he appears to have been unaware of the failure of prohibition in the United States. He considered it immoral for the government to derive revenue from the sale of alcohol (which in India was, like salt, a state monopoly). To compensate for the important loss in revenue caused by the disappearance of excise, he proposed equivalent cuts in the education budget; he thought schools had to do without government subsidies and could live with the sole support of local communities. In reality, the Congress governments faced a difficult situation: they saw their revenue diminish without being able to impose significant cuts in the education budget because of public opposition. Those provincial governments which persisted, after 1947, in implementing prohibition—such as the Madras government or the Gujarat government—failed in their policies, for smuggling developed on a big scale and adulterated alcohol appeared on the black market, leading every year to hundreds of deaths.

Programmes in support of village industries, on the other hand, had some success, in particular in Madras, but they seem to have mostly benefited a strata of merchant-entrepreneurs who put out work to home-based artisans to whom they sold the raw material and from whom they bought the finished product. There was no real revitalization of the village economy of the kind anticipated by Gandhi.

In his lifetime Gandhi was not able to convince even his own political friends of the soundness of his economic programme. In nationalist circles, dominant influences pointed in another direction. Congress leaders such as Jawaharlal Nehru, whose role became increasingly important, were influenced by Keynesian ideas and the Soviet model. They found Gandhi's ideas incompatible with economic realities. Gandhi's difficulty in putting across his economic message was not due to his own dismissive attitude towards economics. For him, economics was a science, but he was critical of dominant neo-classical theories, without however holding Keynesian views. It appears he never paid much attention to Keynes, who is not even mentioned in A.K. Das Gupta's recent study of Gandhi's economic thought.[3]

[3] A.K. Das Gupta, *Gandhi's Economic Thought*, London, 1996.

Gandhi's inability to convince even his closest friends of the soundness of his ideas had probably to do with his failure to present them in a systematic way, exposing him to the risk of being seen as a simple-minded amateur, despite the fact that economics was precisely at the heart of his preoccupations.

Prior to Independence, the Congress Party did not clearly adopt Gandhi's reconstruction programme as its own. When the nationalist party formed in 1938 a National Planning Committee to coordinate the economic policies of the various provincial governments and lay the foundation for planning in a future independent India, it did not really take into account Gandhi's views. There was a de facto coalition between the big Indian industrialists and the Congress Left, represented by Bose and Nehru, both pushing for a policy giving priority to the development of large-scale factories over rural industries. Actually the outlines of India's future economic policy were defined in 1944 in a document known as the 'Bombay Plan', produced by a group of industrialists and economists, without any direct participation by Congress. The blueprint they published advocated a centralized economic model, with a planning which was 'indicative' (in the manner of the French plans) rather than directive and gave priority to heavy industry, holding village industries to be of secondary importance and meant only to remedy localized gaps.

Shortly after the publication of the Bombay Plan, an economist close to the Mahatma published, with the latter's blessing, a so-called 'Gandhian plan' of economic developement,[4] which gave greater importance to rural industries. This plan, not officially endorsed by Congress, had only limited circulation and little impact on the actual planning policies of independent India. An interesting feature of the plan was that, contrary to expectations, it did not completely eschew proposals for the development of large-scale industries. Actually its investment outlays were not wildly different from those in the Bombay Plan, even though agriculture and small industries received more. This tends to show that Gandhi, in the matter of economics, was more realistic than he is credited with being. Although in principle he opposed mechanized industries, he was pragmatic enough to understand that India could not dispense with them.

[4] S.N. Agarwal, *The Gandhian Plan of Economic Development for India*, Bombay, 1944.

In the aftermath of independence Gandhi's ideas were to some extent incorporated into the economic policies followed by India, particularly after 1955. Within the framework of 'Indian socialism', which became the official ideology of Congress, some sectors of the market were specifically earmarked for village industries while others were reserved for big private or public industries. It was more a symbolic homage paid to Gandhi than real commitment to a Gandhian-style programme. Actual results were mixed, and the trend towards industrial concentration was not really reversed, even if slightly attenuated. Often the development of small-scale industries hid practices of subcontracting: part of the production of big textile firms now takes place in small decentralized workshops which are mechanized units (powerlooms), controlled by firms and benefiting from a whole array of fiscal exemptions, which make for large extra profits. The relative failure of policies meant to support small industries cannot be blamed on Gandhi's ideas, inasmuch as these policies were applied in a context completely different from the one Gandhi had in mind.

Gandhi's ideas on society and economy had little impact on his contemporaries; they were taken more seriously only from the 1970s. We find here a typical example of the cyclical nature of intellectual fashions. Gandhi's views originated in a certain intellectual ambience of the late nineteenth and early twentieth centuries but were out of step with the dominant sensibilities of the inter-war years and of the second post-war period, when there was renewed confidence in technical progress and the benefits of industrialization. The Soviet model, in the idealized version given it by the Webbs in their famous book, *The Soviet Union. A New Civilization* (which so influenced Nehru), appeared to offer a way towards progress without some of the costs linked to capitalism and helped to rehabilitate industry in the eyes of a large fraction of the intelligentsia.

Gandhi who, contrary to some of his closest friends, always remained immune to the Soviet model, found himself in disagreement with the leading intelllectual trend precisely at the moment when he assumed a position of political leadership. Such disjunction remained of little consequence during the 1920s and 1930s, because Gandhi's support base among the masses and large sections of the middle classes allowed him this latitude. But in the long term his position was made more fragile as the Indian élite, while ready to see in him a guru and spiritual teacher, never accepted him as an intellectual inspiration and preferred to follow Nehru, who appeared intellectually more solid. Nehru had more confidence in modern technology, though he was neither a pure technocrat nor neglected the importance of villages. He succeeded in giving a greater impression of technical competence than Gandhi and, as a result, the intelligentsia found more substance in his ideas and even used him to justify its rejection of Gandhian ideas. Only in the 1970s, with the advent of a new phase in the cycle, did Gandhi's ideas find new legitimacy. But their practical application was made even more difficult by the legacy of the policies followed during the first three decades of independent India. The 'window of opportunity' which was opened in the 1970s was closed in the early 1990s, when trends towards globalization started appearing. This is not enough to conclude that Gandhi failed as a reformer, but it clearly signals the limits of his actual influence. The same limitations are found in the case of the struggle against untouchability.

Gandhi and the Fight for the Abolition of Untouchability

This complex and controversial question will be dealt with only in its broad outline. Gandhi's position on untouchability was somewhat contradictory, for he defended the caste system, of which untouchability was a structural element,[5] even while wanting to abolish untouchability. This position had its roots partly in Gandhi's personal history: he never understood the feelings of repulsion felt by most caste Hindus towards Untouchables, including within his own family, and he was also influenced by bhakti and its tendency to blur caste distinctions. It is true that, in their practices, bhakti-inspired movements had rarely gone beyond an abstract preaching of equality before God to promote actual social equality. But the theme of the abolition of untouchability was present in social reform movements prior to Gandhi's arrival on the stage. Among Untouchables, a small educated élite had started to emerge and was trying to lead the mass of their caste-fellows in a struggle for dignity and elementary human rights.

[5] On this point, see L. Dumont, *Homo Hierarchicus. The Caste System and its Implications,* Chicago, London, 1980.

From 1924 onwards Gandhi gave the struggle against untouchability a central place in his programme alongside the battle for khadi. He found himself in direct opposition to the radical movements developing among Untouchables themselves which increasingly advocated a complete break with Hinduism. Gandhi's own view was that untouchability was a purely social fact which had nothing to do with religion, and that it was basically a perversion of Hinduism. He saw the Untouchables, whom he called Harijans, as an essential part of the Hindu community. He fought to have them readmitted into mainstream Hinduism and to abolish discriminations against them—such as their being barred from entering Hindu temples, particularly in the south. He thought that if these discriminations were abolished and non-Untouchable Hindus changed their attitude, the problem of untouchability would be on its way to being solved. It would then reduce into a more manageable question of poverty, to be addressed through socio-economic measures.

He found himself in open disagreement with the main leader of the Untouchables, Dr Ambedkar, who advocated self-reliance and the creation of separate electorates as remedies for the ills suffered by his community. The outcome of the open clash between the two men in 1932 has already been mentioned: Ambedkar was embittered by it and became more strident in his denunciation of Gandhi. As a quid pro quo for renouncing separate electorates, Untouchable leaders obtained some concessions which, later, were incorporated into the 1950 Indian constitution, of which Ambedkar was one of the most important framers.

The text of the constitution was fairly ambiguous: it outlawed untouchability and all the legal disabilities founded on caste but granted Scheduled Castes some specific advantages, such as the reservation of a certain number of seats in parliament, and jobs in the public services. Debates rage over whether these measures really helped the social promotion of the Untouchables in general, or benefited only a small élite to the detriment of the greatest number. I shall only draw attention to the fact that Gandhi's action, whatever its weaknesses and lapses, contributed decisively to giving the question of untouchability central place in the Indian political debate, whereas it had earlier held only a very marginal place.

It could be said that there was a kind of dialectical relationship between Gandhi and Ambedkar, in spite of their personal opposition and differences in views; but for Gandhi, it is not very likely that Ambedkar would have acceded to the status of one of the 'fathers of the nation' which he acquired and which constitutes a precious resource in the struggle of Dalits for dignity and equality in contemporary India. This is however not a view which Dalits accept; there is among them a strong rejection of Gandhi's ideas, which they consider patronizing, and there are growing demands for their complete separation from Hindus. On the other hand, there is less controversy over the fact that Gandhi's action did little to transform in depth the attitudes of Indian society with regard to Untouchables. Although the latter have been recognized equal before the law and benefited from measures of social advancement, in most villages they remain subject to severe discrimination, and, when they attempt at organizing themselves to defend their rights, they often meet with violent repression from upper-caste Hindus, with the complicity of the police and political authorities. Gandhi tried to fight a prejudice which was and remains deeply entrenched. Even if he had only limited success, he contributed to delegitimizing the anti-Untouchable discourse. At least in speech and rhetoric, no Indian politician can now afford to be seen as favouring untouchability.

CHAPTER 7

Gandhi in the Time-frame of Indian History

G andhi's historical role brings out the paradox of a very singular, even frankly eccentric individual who was capable of representing the deepest aspirations of hundreds of millions of men and women with whom he had actually very little in common. The encounter between the man and his people, at a very special moment in the history of both, is what constitutes the enigma of Gandhi. But first let us try to situate Gandhi in the more general context of Indian intellectual history.

Between Victorian Intellectual and Neo-traditionalist Hindu

Two very different readings of Gandhi's position in the field of intellectual history have been put forward, and they will be examined here, not for their intrinsic value, but because of the light they throw on him. The first, which takes into account Gandhi's intellectual formation, the authors he read, and the influences he acknowledged, places him squarely within the anti-modernist trend of thought which developed in Europe from the middle of the nineteenth century, around John Ruskin, Edward Carpenter and Leo Tolstoi. The second lays more emphasis on his links to a specifically Indian reformist trend inaugurated by Rammohun Roy and continued by Ramakrishna, Sri Aurobindo and Vivekananda. These two readings are not mutually exclusive. Gandhi himself recognized the intellectual debt he owed to the West and to men like Ruskin and Tolstoi, but he also stressed the indigenous sources of his thought. He viewed the existence of a strata of anglicized intellectuals as one of the most tragic consequences of the colonization of India and wanted to differentiate himself clearly from that group. The real question is not however whether Gandhi was anglicized or not; he was a Victorian intellectual rather than an anglicized one, and he himself did not realize to what extent, intellectually, he was a product of the Victorian era.

There is nothing surprising in the fact that Gandhi, who was born in 1869, was deeply influenced by the intellectual ambience of the late Victorian period. His intellect took shape in the colonial context of South Africa, rather different from that of India because it was more directly subject to the influence of the metropolis. Gandhi's view of the world was influenced by the radical critique of industrial modernity from the ethical and aesthetic points of view which had been put forward in England in the second half of the nineteenth century. While in London, Gandhi came under the spell of these ideas, and their impact led him to become a vegetarian; the rationalization and refining of his vegetarianism remained a major intellectual preoccupation throughout his life. In South Africa, through his reading and frequenting of European intellectual circles directly influenced by dominant trends in Britain, he deepened his knowledge of European anti-modernist thought. Through his friend Polak he discovered Ruskin, a most central figure in nineteenth-century British intellectual life who was, at the same time the great ancestor of British socialism and the art and craft movement, and famous both for his defence of medievalism in art and his critique of industrial civilization. In 1904 Gandhi wrote a Gujarati paraphrase of Ruskin's most famous book, *Unto his Last*, and called it *Sarvodaya*.

The most important idea Gandhi borrowed from Ruskin was that economics could not be separated from ethics. Beyond this, the exact nature of Ruskin's influence over Gandhi remains a matter of controversy. Gandhi was more *directly* influenced by 'New Age' thinkers such as Edward Carpenter, the eccentric who preached a subversion of traditional morals through the practice of sublimated homosexuality, as well as vegetarianism, naturopathy, and opposition to vaccination. Upholders of 'New Age' views refused the conformism and uniformity of modern life and advocated regression to a more 'natural' lifestyle. The critique of modern civilization contained in *Hind Swaraj* is largely rooted in these ideas, and Gandhi did not go back on these. In 1909, the year he wrote *Hind Swaraj*, he became a member of the South African chapter of the Union of Ethical Societies,[1] a kind of think-tank created in England in 1896 aimed at giving religion a scientific base, promoting the role of morality in political life, and making philosophy an anthropocentric synthesis. Many prominent Victorian intellectuals, such as the future Labour Prime Minister Ramsay MacDonald, belonged to this association, which supported the struggle of the Indians of South Africa and had a significant degree of influence in Britain.

Gandhi was in short a full-fledged member of the imperial intelligentsia of the late Victorian and Edwardian era. This is seen most clearly in his relation to science. Contrary to the widely held view, Gandhi was not hostile to science as a mode of thought, even if he was sceptical about the usefulness of many of its discoveries and himself displayed little scientific curiosity. His ability to combine, to a certain extent, a scientific turn of mind and a stand against modernity reflects traits of a specifically Victorian notion of science. For the Victorians, science was very directly linked to emotions and ethics.[2] The cult of truth which characterized Victorian scientific thought was also a cult of nature and closely related to morals. The great mathematician W.K. Clifford argued that it was immoral to conduct one's life on the basis of beliefs which were not empirically grounded. Victorians thought that nature itself, knowledge of which was the object of science, provided a norm of truth, and that the acceptance of such a norm was the key to effective moral action. For such people, comprehending objective laws which regulated natural phenomena allowed one to understand the laws of human behaviour. The statement of a scientific vulgarizer, Edward Clodd—'In proving the unvarying relation between cause and effect in morals as in physics, science gives the clue to the remedy for moral ills'[3]—could have been Gandhi's.

For the Victorians, knowledge of the laws of nature also helped develop oneness with it. Victorian science stressed the basic unity

[1] M. Green, *Gandhi, Voice of a New Age Revolution*, op. cit.

[2] On these questions, see T. Cosslett, *The 'Scientific Movement' and Victorian Literature*, Brighton, 1982.

[3] B.E. Clodd, *The Story of Creation: A Plain Account of Evolution*, London, 1888, p. 222.

between different forms of life, organic as well as inorganic. Its concept of the universe was holistic rather than mechanistic and, to a large extent, accorded with Gandhi's philosophical convictions. Gandhi saw in science a norm of truth and a model of self-discipline. He had an experimentalist notion of science: one of the key words in his discourse was 'experiment', as in the title of his autobiography. Experiment implied a laboratory, and 'laboratory' was a central metaphor in Gandhi's writings. He saw his own self as a laboratory for experiments with truth, he viewed his ashram as a laboratory for experiments on social relations, and he treated India as a laboratory to test the validity of the doctrine of satyagraha.

He often talked of the science of satyagraha. According to him, satyagraha was governed by objective laws, independent of the will of participants: if the satyagrahi was not pure of heart, he would fail, whatever his efforts; conversely, if his actions were inspired by pure feelings he would succeed and overcome all obstacles. In Gandhian thought there is this complex mix of objectivism and subjectivism.

The widely held view of Gandhi as an enemy of science comes from the confusion between science and technology. Gandhi was a severe critic of the ways in which scientific discoveries were applied in the medical and industrial fields, but his critique did not extend to science itself. On the contrary he viewed science as providing a norm of truth because it was based on experimentation. He wanted to introduce the experimental method into his private and political life. He did not conceive of truth that was not based on experimentation. One might even question if Gandhi's God was transcendent, since he believed so strongly in truth only through experimentation. It is easy to be dismissive of his notion of science, which happily mixed Victorian ideas with notions inherited from traditional Indian systems of thought, but it would be a grave error to see him as an anti-rationalist thinker. In fact a close look at the enormous corpus of his writings on the subject of dietetics, and a consideration of his obstinate quest for the most rational diet lead to the inescapable conclusion that he was hyper-rationalist.

Another crucial influence on Gandhi was Tolstoi, and his anarchist brand of Christian socialism. While in South Africa, Gandhi exchanged voluminous correspondence with the Russian writer and Tolstoi's ideas about religion helped him bridge the gap between Christianity and the Hindu tradition—which he discovered late. Two texts, the *Bhagavad Gita* and the *Ramayana* (Tulsidas's version), became essential references for him. From these he borrowed in particular the idea of the sovereignty of the mind over passions, which came to be at the heart of his political philosophy.

To delineate the broad outlines of Gandhi's often complex and contradictory thought, there is no choice but to start with *Hind Swaraj*,[4] the only theoretical text he ever wrote, even if it was merely a stage in the development of his thought. First written in Gujarati and then translated into English by Gandhi himself to give it wider circulation and allow it to reach a British public, this takes the form of a dialogue between a reader, represented by an Indian youth attracted to revolutionary terrorism, and an editor, who is Gandhi himself. The dialogue reveals, apart from a reading of Plato,[5] Gandhi's didactic purpose. In London, during a few weeks' stay, Gandhi had been in contact with Indian revolutionary circles then under the spell of the Maharashtrian intellectual V.D. Savarkar, later notorious as the ideologue of Hindu nationalism. Gandhi was convinced that the ideas and the deeds of revolutionary terrorists (such as the killing of Sir Curzon Wyllie by Madanlal Dhingra) were a 'mortal danger' for India. His pamphlet aimed primarily at detaching educated Indian youth from the influence of terrorists, though this did not prevent the book from being considered subversive by the colonial authorities, and banned from the country—an interdiction lifted only in 1919.

In the book Gandhi is led to broaden his scope to encompass a global critique of the terrorist ideology. He sees it as based in essence on blind faith in technical progress and brutal force, an ideology dominant in the West which was in the process of invading India with potentially devastating consequences. Gandhi was drawn into conducting a global critical survey of modern civilization, a central part of the text, and this critique is the main reason why Gandhi is considered an enemy of modernity. While he never reneged on *Hind Swaraj*, he did nuance

[4] The best available edition is Gandhi, *Hind Swaraj and other Writings*, edited by A.J. Parel, Cambridge, 1997.

[5] Gandhi wrote a Gujarati paraphrase of *The Apology of Socrat*. See Iyer, *The Moral and Political Thought*, op. cit., p. 10.

some of his statements. It would be misleading to analyse the text as a manifesto against Western modernity, without keeping in mind the very specific context in which it was written.

Gandhi's target was modern civilization and its consequences for both England and India, which for him were not fundamentally different: for England, as much as India, was a victim of it. Gandhi's view was that Home Rule, the aim of revolutionaries, would be pointless and devoid of emancipatory value if unaccompanied by a complete reversal of the principles regulating society. He wanted to work for the kind of swaraj which would bring true moral and political liberation to India and Britain. This implied a total reversal of values, and it meant emphasizing the role of dharma, i.e. the antitheses of the greed that characterized modern industrial civilization.

Unlike other Indian nationalist thinkers, in particular those who operated within the framework of Hindu neo-traditionalist thought, Gandhi did not believe in the intrinsic superiority of Indian over Western civilization. He did not essentialize the West even while he was critical of its blind faith in material progress and of its cult of violence. He believed that some values lost in the West had been preserved in India and that India offered the West a chance of regeneration, provided India itself did not succumb to the blandishments of modern industrial civilization, as desired by its young revolutionaries. In saving India from the devastating consequences of modern industrialization Gandhi hoped to save the West from its own demons and give mankind a chance to rediscover true values. It was mostly the spiritual emptiness of modern civilization which frightened Gandhi.

He refined the general critique of modern civilization developed by Ruskin and Tolstoi by incorporating into this an analysis of the West's pernicious influence on non-Western countries such as India. He also relied on the critique of the economic impact of British rule put forward by Dadabhai Naoroji and other nationalist authors. More fundamentally, Gandhi criticized modern civilization in the name of a non-exclusivist spirituality rooted in the Indian context. Gandhi's critique of the modern West was therefore predicated on both an internal and an external point of view. This was the source of its strength, while it also gave rise to many misunderstandings.

The originality of Gandhi's position lies in his conception of morality, which gives central place to the notion of truth, rather than to

that of conformity to religious norms, even those of the Hindu tradition. Gandhi used the latter in a partly strategic way; he saw it as a
precious resource for the critique of Western modernity but he did not
make it the measure of all things. Gandhi's quest for truth led him to
take positions which appear eccentric to posterity—such as his opposition to vaccination and his preference for naturopathy, which led
him to reject not only Western medicine but also Indian traditional
medicine, both ayurvedic and yunani. His anti-conformism sometimes
also resulted in very enlightened views, as when he questioned the
authority of the Shastras when it appeared to him that they went
against universal moral principles. He used this argument, in particular,
against those who claimed shastric authority to justify untouchability.
For him, religion had meaning only if it was consistent with morality.
The laws of the physical and mental universe had the same character,
he did not see morals as subject to cultural relativism, but rather as
the same in all cultures. For him Hinduism, as a true religion, could
not include prescriptions that did not conform to universal morality:
those were the result of accretions and interpolations.

The very specific mixture of modern and traditional ideas found in
Gandhi struck many commentators as odd. An interesting reading was
put forward by the Rudolphs, who saw Gandhi as an instance of the
'modernity of tradition'.[6] In their view, Gandhi's success in modernizing Indian political life through a largely traditional idiom, had its
source in the fact that there already existed in pre-colonial India
organizational techniques, such as those used by bhakti movements,
which could be redeployed in the management of modern political
organizations. It could be added that some of the ancestral values held
by Hindu merchant castes were not very different from those of the
middle classes of Victorian England, in particular as far as the domestic economy was concerned.

But there is no need to obliterate Gandhi's Victorian side. It was
most visible in some of the principles guiding his private and public
life, which in turn influenced the movements he conducted. Gandhi's
Victorianism is particularly evident in his relationship to time and

---

[6] Lloyd I. Rudolph and Susan H. Rudolph, 'The Traditional Roots of
Charisma: Gandhi', in *The Modernity of Tradition: Political Development in
India,* Chicago and London, 1967, pp. 155–249.

to work, which was a clear break with practices widespread in Indian political circles. The time discipline introduced in everyday life by the Industrial Revolution was one of the most important transformations to have taken place in England during the Victorian era. That discipline had been introduced into India most particularly with the building of the first railways, but it had not spread far and wide, largely because of the very limited and haphazard character of Indian colonial industrialization. Political life followed its own lazy rhythm and pre-1914 Congress leaders, either of the Gokhale or the Tilak school, had adopted a style which was fairly relaxed and nonchalant. In 1917, when Tilak arrived half an hour late at a meeting, he was brusquely reprimanded by Gandhi who declared that if one did not bother about keeping time at meetings, one should not wonder at seeing swaraj delayed.

Gandhi introduced a completely different style in this sphere of Indian political life. He substituted nonchalance with a rigorous management of time, surpassing that of many British politicians. Punctuality was an obsession with him and, in the inventory of his possessions made after his death, a large watch figured as the only thing of value he owned. His days were organized according to a very strict schedule which rarely changed: he rose around 4 a.m. and went to bed around 9 p.m., which meant a seventeen-hour day with only a few breaks for prayers. Gandhi tried to stick to his schedule and tolerated very few diversions. In the pre-Gandhian era, Indian political leaders used to hold a more or less permanent durbar, in the way of Mughal emperors, and it was easy to reach them even without an appointment. Gandhi's day was organized so that a few hours were specifically reserved for appointments, which had to be made in advance, even if he was not utterly inflexible over these. He adopted a deliberately non-royal style and was a model of efficiency. He lost no time gossiping and, each day, with the help of a well-organized secretariat, could achieve an enormous amount of work. In this area too he was a great modernizer and broke with tradition most conspicuously.

Gandhi thus introduced into Indian political life Victorian values such as economy, financial transparency, and a rational use of time. His predecessors had rejected these as too British and therefore unworthy of patriotic Indians. Gandhi succeeded in 'naturalizing' these values, in making them accepted as Indian, disabusing the idea of them as the product of servile imitation. Inasmuch as these Victorian values were basically bourgeois values, the question arises whether Gandhi transformed the Indian nationalist movement into a bourgeois movement. Was he the agent of a bourgeois hegemony over India's nationalist movement?

Gandhi and Bourgeois Nationalism

There are several possible ways of looking at the relationship between Gandhi and the Indian bourgeoisie. For a long time it was an accepted truth among Indian Marxists that Gandhi was simply a bourgeois nationalist. He was denounced as a particularly pernicious bourgeois agent because of his capacity to clothe his bourgeois programme in a populist language susceptible of misleading the masses. This was, in particular, the view of Rajani Palme Dutt. This view of Gandhi was too divorced from the truth of Gandhi's actions to be sustainable in the long term. In the 1960s and 1970s some Indian nationalist historians, such as Bipan Chandra, influenced by Marxism, put forward another reading of the relationship between Gandhi and the bourgeoisie. Now Gandhi was the instigator of a class front, in which the bourgeoisie necessarily had a leading role, but this front drew its essential strength from its capacity to mobilize large strata of the Indian people to implement its principal tasks, namely an anti-imperialist and anti-feudal, bourgeois democratic revolution. These historians used the evidence of the close links which existed between Gandhi and Indian business circles to make him the true political representative of a rising Indian capitalist class, ignoring the equally ample evidence that the relationship between Gandhi and the Indian capitalists was characterized by a high degree of ambiguity.[7] In the 1980s a different approach became more popular among Indian Marxists. There was now a recognition that Gandhi's thought and action had been often misinterpreted and that the peasantry had been able to find in Gandhi a genuine voice. Influenced by Gramsci's views, some of these historians, gathered into the original Subaltern Studies collective, presented

[7] On this point, see C. Markovits, *Indian Business and Nationalist Politics 1931–1939: The Indigenous Capitalist Class and the Rise of the Congress Party,* Cambridge, 1985.

India's struggle for independence as the example of a 'passive revolution' in which the peasant masses had been mobilized yet prevented from acquiring real initiative.[8] For those who held this view, Gandhi's specific role had been to define a form of struggle in which the masses participated but were subjected to close control and so could not define the objectives which were specifically their own. For these historians, Gandhi had channellized the often confused aspirations of the masses and fashioned them so as to make them compatible with the implementation of a programme which was basically bourgeois. He had opened the possibility of an appropriation of mass struggle by bourgeois elements but had not necessarily been the main agent of this appropriation, which had been more the work of his lieutenants—such as Patel and Nehru. These historians at least implicitly recognized the existence of a spectrum of historical possibilities in Gandhism and explained the final, although partial, triumph of the bourgeoisie in terms of the specific balance of forces which existed in India in the 1930s and 1940s, and of the weakness of the left and the Communists.

Beyond these changing appreciations by Indian Marxists, it must be kept in mind that it was through the agency of Gandhi, rather than of the members of the Indian bourgeoisie, that some 'bourgeois' values (understood in a fairly general sense) gained acceptance in India. Indian capitalists, generally issued from the Hindu merchant castes, often had a behaviour and mindset which were not very 'bourgeois'. Bourgeois values were better represented among Parsi industrialists, such as the Tata family, but they remained aloof for a long time from the nationalist movement because of their loyalist attachment to the British Crown. Gandhi's bourgeois side was manifest mostly in his way of managing the nationalist movement—more than in the objectives he gave to the movement, which were not very specifically bourgeois, even if they took into account the interests of the bourgeoisie.

In the management of the movements he directed, Gandhi introduced principles of transparency unknown before. All expenses had to be justified and a detailed balance sheet kept on a daily basis. Gandhi brought open economic calculation, a consideration of cost–benefit,

[8] See P. Chatterjee, 'Gandhi and the Critique of Civil Society', in R. Guha (ed.), *Subaltern Studies III. Writings on South Asian History and Society*, Delhi, 1984, pp. 153–95.

into the political realm. This calculating aspect of his personality is not always clearly perceived, but it emerges from a close analysis of the movements he inspired and led. In the same vein, he was able to give negotiation a more positive meaning in the Indian political lexicon. Prior to Gandhi, negotiation with the colonizer was seen either as sheer bargaining or as a demonstration of weakness, the sign of a deep inferiority complex. Gandhi imposed the idea that Indians could negotiate on an equal footing with the colonial government, without loss of prestige, and make concessions without necessarily being considered cowards. The idea of 'give and take', foreign to traditional political mentality, acquired an aura of legitimacy which it has retained and which partly accounts for the 'civil' character of Indian political life (which does not of course prevent violence and devious manoeuvrings).

There is, in this respect, a striking difference between Indian and Pakistani political cultures, although they are born of the same matrix, and it shows the durable impact that the 'naturalization' of some Victorian notions by Gandhi had over Indian politics. 'Give and take' is very directly linked to 'fair play', another essential trait of Victorian mentality. In spite of wearing a loincloth, Gandhi remained till the end of his life, in some respects, a Victorian gentleman, and he naturalized into the Indian context certain behavioural norms of gentlemanly conduct. Thanks to him, it was possible to behave like a gentleman without being denounced as a servile imitator of the colonizer. By introducing rational calculation and fair play into political life, Gandhi contributed to an acclimatization of bourgeois values (in their most general sense) in the Indian context. Yet he was not a spokesman for any particular social strata of the Indian population. This was both his main weakness and his principal strength. If he had no solid social base to rely upon in all circumstances, he was not the prisoner of a specific group either, and could thus represent different aspirations at different moments.

The Nature of Gandhi's Charisma

Gandhi's leadership clearly belongs within the category of 'charismatic' in the Weberian typology. Gandhi's charisma was, however, of a very different nature from that of other leaders of the Third World in the twentieth century. He had neither the prestige of the military leader that Ho Chi Minh had, nor the aura of the tribune like Sukarno, nor the reputation for theoretical intelligence as in Mao Zedong. His speeches were in the nature of conversations with the crowd and were always didactic in intent. But as a teacher he did not lord over his pupils, in the manner of many Indian middle-class politicians. He knew how to meet his audience on equal terms and was not bothered with considerations of social etiquette. The magic of Gandhi's word operated through the special radiance of his personality rather than the specific content of his speeches, which were often freely interpreted by the audience. What mattered to them was to see him and hear him; the details of what he said were much less important. His influence did not come from a process of self-identification: although he sought to dress as a peasant, Indian peasants were never fooled into believing he was one of them. Had it been so, they would not have followed him and loved him the way they did. He knew how to give audiences a sense of collective identity, beyond considerations of caste, creed or region. Those who listened to the Mahatma felt that they belonged to one national community whether they were the humblest of peasants or lawyers or traders; social distinctions were abolished, the dream of the nation was becoming flesh. Gandhi thus gave meaning to a mass of vague and often contradictory aspirations.

In an earlier chapter, we examined the image of Gandhi among Indian peasants, but what needs explaining is how, beyond the level of representations, Gandhi was able to shake up the world of the Indian countryside out of its torpor and make it a full participant in a nationalist struggle—from which it had previously kept aloof. This remains a puzzling phenomenon. It is specially difficult to measure the impact that Gandhi's socio-economic programme had upon the peasantry, even though it was explicitly directed towards the economic rehabilitation of the countryside. How did peasants react to Gandhi's message about the necessary rebirth of village industries and the promotion of khadi? There is ample evidence that this had more impact on the urban middle classes than on the peasantry. Given the high cost of khadi, only relatively affluent peasants, such as the Patidars of Gujarat, could switch to it; the bulk of the peasantry did not change its consumption habits to answer the call of the Mahatma.

Nor do Gandhi's admonishments in the matter of hygiene and sanitation appear to have made headway. In the same way, his anti-untouchability work had more success in the towns and cities than in the countryside, where it remained largely ignored. What Indian peasants retained from Gandhi's message was mostly that they were part of the nation and that it could not be built to their exclusion. Gandhi gave them a dignity which no other politician had done. He called on their participation within the national struggle in a language they could understand, even if his words did not always have the same meaning to them as they did to Gandhi. For the sake of this recognition of their humanity and their citizenship, Gandhi earned immense gratitude from them. He himself often complained of the excessive love the masses had for him, but it is this relationship of love which holds the key to the rapport between Gandhi and the peasantry. The mental structures of bhakti no doubt favoured this kind of relationship between the people and a man whom they saw as endowed with divine powers. But why were Indian peasants particularly ready to receive the Gandhian revelation in the 1920s?

Gandhi and the Expectations of the Peasantry

1920 represents in many ways a watershed in the history of the Indian countryside. This was the time when a process of transition had started away from a demographic *ancien régime*, characterized by high fertility and high mortality, towards a new régime defined by a fall in mortality rates. It resulted in an acceleration of demographic growth, which, combined with the increasing shortage of cultivable land, ushered in a potential Malthusian scenario. The 1920-47 period in the Indian countryside was one of rampant agrarian crisis, aggravated from 1926 onwards by the fall in agricultural prices; this reached catastrophic proportions in the early 1930s with the onset of the world Depression. That crisis affected all strata of the peasantry, in particular the 'middle' peasantry which sold part of its produce on the market and felt the full impact of the fall in prices. This strata, rather than agricultural labourers—often Untouchables, who accounted for the bulk of the really poor—was the one which showed greatest interest in the Gandhian message.

His call to dignity and self-sufficiency also met with a particular response among the fairly educated peasants who had regular contacts with towns and cities. Social reform movements had been active among them for decades, and they were therefore receptive to the social reformist aspect of the Gandhian programme, such as the struggle against alcoholism. Among the agrarian communities which showed themselves susceptible to Gandhian influence, the Patidars of Kheda district in Gujarat deserve special mention. Vallabhbhai Patel, himself a Patidar, played a large part in spreading Gandhi's message among them. Overall, though, if Gandhi became a figure of hope for the peasant masses in a broader sense, it was not so much because of his programme, of which only bits reached them, but because they projected on him millennarian expectations which had been deeply buried in their consciousness and awaited an opportunity to come out in the open.

These expectations had expressed themselves in the course of various risings in the 1858–1920 period, but they gathered increased strength and took on a pan-Indian dimension in 1920, when rumours endowed the Mahatma with miraculous powers. Many now thought that the time had come for the kingdom of justice to be established in India, which Gandhi called Ramraj. Such hopes expressed themselves fully during non-cooperation, and, even after its abandonment, they remained linked in the minds of many to the person of Gandhi. They continued to burst forth sporadically during the 1920s, taking the form of localized agitations led by charismatic leaders who were seen as little Gandhis.

During Civil Disobedience, the economic woes suffered by the peasantry because of the Depression provided fertile ground for the diffusion of the Gandhian message, but the existence, in some areas, of well-entrenched groups of Gandhian activists allowed for a better control and prevented excesses. In the 1930s there developed in some regions peasant organizations—Kisan Sabhas—mostly strong among middle peasants; these could be used as a relay, but they were not always easy to control, especially when activists who were close to the left gained positions of influence in them. On the whole, Gandhi found in the countryside the base he needed to develop his movements, but more durable forms of organization, capable of giving a coherent direction to peasant struggles, did not really emerge. For many Indian peasants Gandhi remained a kind of messiah, not so much because of his concrete programme but because of the miraculous powers rumour endowed him with, stoking the millennarian aspirations of a largely illiterate peasantry.

The encounter between the figure of the Mahatma and the expectations of the peasantry which occurred around 1920 had a lasting impact. Even if it was partly based on a misunderstanding on the part of peasants, who often thought that Gandhi wanted to subvert the established social order in the countryside—which was far from his intentions—it gives a key to Gandhi's exceptional popularity in the countryside and to the lasting domination he could establish over the nationalist movement.

The manner in which Gandhi could answer the demands of his peasant followers was through his adoption of an idiom and style which answered the idea they had of a charismatic saviour. But how was he able to channellize such expectations? A measure of his success is given by a comparison between the hasty withdrawal of non-cooperation in 1922, following Chauri-Chaura, and the much more gradual retreat from Civil Disobedience in 1931–4. In 1922, Gandhi had no choice but to suddenly stop the movement, because he was afraid that a frustration of the expectations of the peasantry he had himself kindled would result in violent risings which he could not prevent, as he did not have a hard core of disciples entrenched in the countryside. In 1931–4, he was able to achieve a kind of 'soft landing', because he could rely on a network of rural activists which partly channellized the energies released by Civil Disobedience into the constructive programme. Civil Disobedience had not, it is true, given rise to the same kind of expectations as non-cooperation, and had not therefore radicalized the peasantry to the same extent, but it was largely thanks to its impact that the Congress won the 1937 elections in most provinces. It captured the rural vote, which was mostly that of middle and rich peasants (the poor had not gained the franchise yet). From this time on, the movement entered a trajectory of institutionalization which Gandhi did not completely master, but which he set in motion. Bourgeois rationality had triumphed over peasant millennarianism, without which it could not have instituted itself in the first place.

It must be recognized that, beyond his own intentions, Gandhi was the catalyst of a process of 'normalization' in which the expectations of the Indian peasantry were instrumentalized in the service of a transition which was fundamentally of a 'bourgeois' character. However, in the course of this, not everything constituting popular aspirations to a fairer order got lost; through the constructive programme, the seed of potential dissent was sown and this has remained to haunt the Indian bourgeois state. It is worth noting that in a speech delivered on the occasion of the fiftieth anniversary of the proclamation of the Republic, on 26 January 2000, the President of India, K.R. Narayanan, in a hard-hitting survey of the achievements and failures of the Indian state, claimed that Gandhi's constructive programme could still be of use as a guide towards more social justice.

Gandhi's most specific contribution to Indian history is the synthesis he was able to achieve between peasant millennarianism and bourgeois rationality. His ability to reach that synthesis had historical roots. India, in the first half of the twentieth century can be described as a 'nation-in-formation'. Its British rulers, on the basis of given facts, such as India's enormous ethnic, religious and linguistic diversity, denied India the status of a 'nation' in the European sense of the term, meaning a relatively homogeneous ensemble. The nationalists retorted by painting India as a fairly homogeneous nation in which divisions were only superficial. But before Gandhi came on the scene, their nation was an empty shell, unrecognized as such by those hundreds of millions of peasants who, despite lectures by urban politicians, did not see beyond the horizons of their own village. India was the shadow of a nation, a series of dots on a map, a virtual nation whose unity was only negative: the fascinated hatred for a conqueror. Gandhi—not alone, but with all those he persuaded and influenced—transformed this virtual nation into a real one.

This he achieved primarily by his capacity to integrate peasant expectations into the struggle for dignity and national independence. The absorption of millennarianism into a movement founded on bourgeois rationality, and on a realistic appreciation of the balance of forces, is a rather unique phenomenon. In most other countries, bourgeois rationality developed in direct opposition to peasant aspirations. In India, Gandhi was able to effect a kind of synthesis between two historically opposed forces.

Some factors favoured his success: the bourgeoisie did not enjoy a position of hegemony at the economic, social and cultural levels, because of its relative weakness and its extreme segmentation, which left open a space for peasant millennarianism to deploy itself, even though on its own it had no political outlet. Besides, there did not exist in India sufficiently organized revolutionary forces capable of using peasant aspirations to their own purposes, as in China and Vietnam. In such a situation, the stalemate could only be broken if there arose a leader capable of capturing the energies of the peasantry without directly subordinating them to the objectives of the bourgeoisie. That was Gandhi's achievement. He gave the peasantry the possibility of participating in the national struggle without abandoning its millennarian modes of thought and action, which he redirected around his own charismatic personality.

The British were deprived of their most potent anti-nationalist argument, i.e. that nationalism was a purely urban movement, not supported by the mass of peasants, and therefore devoid of representative character. To maintain their rule, they resorted to 'divide and rule' tactics, benefiting from the fact that part of the élite chose to play the game of communalism. There remains, however, the inescapable fact that Gandhi could never convince the Muslim peasantry that they were part of the nation as much as their Hindu counterparts. The reason may have been that, among the Muslims, millennarianism always had strong religious overtones, and Gandhi himself was too 'secular' to know how to deal with such movements. Gandhi's nation remained in this sense, primarily a nation of Hindus.

CHAPTER 8

Gandhi and Non-violence

In modern societies confronting an increasing level of violence, Gandhi's image as an apostle of non-violence is undoubtedly the major source of his lasting popularity. The question arises of the relevance of that image, and this chapter looks at Gandhi's theory and practice of non-violence.

Non-violent Resistance: Gandhi's Contribution

While acknowledging his debt to Thoreau and Tolstoi at the level of ideas, Gandhi did not hesitate to present himself as the inventor of a radically new form of non-violent struggle, which he took great care to distinguish from 'passive resistance'. To signal the difference, he forged the term 'satyagraha', which gave an Indian and 'spiritual' connotation to a form of struggle which was already part of the political répertoire in the English-speaking countries. When Gandhi launched his first South African campaign in 1907, he was not perceived as a radical innovator. His struggle appeared to fit within a well-established political tradition in Anglo-American history, which went back to the 1830s, to the foundation in Boston by William Lloyd Garrison and his friends of the 'Non-Resistance Society' to fight slavery by non-violent means. The society's 'declaration of principles', in spite of its use of an evangelical language, was certainly not a plea for passivity.[1] A few years later, in a well-known text of 1849, Thoreau put forward a theory of civil disobedience which made its mark on political philosophy and practice.[2] During the second half of the nineteenth century, there were examples of non-violent struggles waged by English and American

---

[1] See the text in P. Meyer (ed.), *The Pacifist Conscience*, London, 1966, pp. 124–8.

[2] For a recent analysis, see the Introduction in N.L. Rosenblum (ed.), *Thoreau: Political Writings*, Cambridge, 1996.

Quakers. Perusal of a recent bibliography of studies on non-viol-ence[3] shows that the field was broader than is often realized and that Gandhi's place in it was not as central as is generally assumed. He cer-tainly did not have a foundational role.

It is sometimes underlined that Gandhi was the first to have launched non-violent struggles on a massive scale. But even this point is open to debate.[4] Gandhi's genius lay rather in his ability to achieve a pragmatic synthesis between diverse forms of struggle, such as individual or collective fasting, boycott and civil disobedience, which had been preached and practised by different groups at different moments in time. He gathered them all under the rather mysterious term of satyagraha and linked this technique of struggle with the aspirations of Indians to be free of British domination. It is largely this ability to enlarge a form of struggle which had been used mostly by small groups to the context of a mass nationalist struggle that makes Gandhi the architect of a whole new kind of non-violent resistance. This point appears more important than the question of the originality of Gandhi's philosophical position, which has attracted a lot of at-tention but over which no clear consensus has emerged.

It is, however, debatable whether the success gained by the Congress under Gandhi's leadership in the struggle for Indian independence without the use of armed violence is to be explained primarily by the form of struggle chosen, or by the context and content of the move-ment. The simple fact that success was never replicated on a similar scale elsewhere tends to point to the latter hypothesis, unless one chooses to put forward an 'essentialist' thesis on the fundamentally non-violent nature of Indian civilization—but that view is defended by no serious author.[5] As a recent scholarly work suggests, it was the

[3] R.M. McCarthy and G. Sharp, *Non Violent Action: A Research Guide*, London and New York, 1997.

[4] Of particular relevance here is the 'O Le Mau' movement of the inhabitants of Western Samoa launched in 1918 to protest the mandate given by the League of Nations to New Zealand. That movement, under the leadership of chief Tamasese, was characterized by its mass character and the absence of violence. See M.J. Field, *Mau: Samoa's Struggle against New Zealand Oppression*, Wellington, 1984.

[5] On this point, see D. Vidal, G. Tarabout and E. Meyer, 'Introduction: Pour une interprétation des notions de violence et de non-violence dans l'hindouisme

loss of the social meaning of violence induced by the disarming of the warrior castes effected by British power which created the space within which Gandhian non-violence could deploy itself.[6] The emergence of Gandhi as a non-violent leader must be re-placed within a given historical context: it is not the function of a particular religious and cultural predisposition of Indian society towards the use of such methods. The choice of non-violent methods by the Indian nationalist movement is to be primarily explained by a combination of factors which were specific to India in the 1920–47 period, a point taken up later in some detail. The contrast between Gandhian non-violent prescriptions and the reality of mass violence in post-Independence India—from the massacres of Partition in 1947–8 to the destruction of the Babri Masjid in 1992, through various episodes of violence against Muslims and the anti-Sikh riots of 1984, not to mention other phenomena of violence in everyday social relations—has become a kind of topos. Although the interpretation of those facts is far from obvious and falls outside the scope of this book, it has to be recognized that they tend to relativize Gandhi's impact and locate him within a well-defined historical niche.

From Satyagraha to Non-violence: A Gandhian Itinerary

Starting with an essentially pragmatic use of already well-known techniques of struggle, Gandhi progressed towards the enunciation of a very general philosophy, never presented in a systematic form. This has given rise to many comments and there remains some ambiguity due to terminological uncertainties. The term 'non-violence' is used in a fairly undifferentiated way by commentators, while Gandhi himself used three different terms: the Sanskrit word ahimsa, central to Jaina doctrine, which means a refusal to harm life in any form (including animal life, which explains why pious Jains wear a mask to

---

et dans la société indienne', in D. Vidal, G. Tarabout and E. Meyer (eds), *Violences et non-violences en Inde, Purusartha, 16*, pp. 9–21.

    [6] See D. Vidal, *Violence and Truth. A Rajasthani Kingdom Confronts Colonial Authority*, Delhi, 1997.

avoid inadvertently swallowing small insects); satyagraha, a neologism forged by Gandhi by combining the Sanskrit words *satya* (truth), and *agraha* (to hold firmly to), which is generally translated as truth force or soul force; and finally the fairly neutral English term 'non-violence'. Even in his English writings, Gandhi rarely used the last, preferring to use satyagraha when he referred to specific movements and ahimsa when he discussed religious and philosophical matters. His own use, actually, was not devoid of ambiguity, as shown by a comparison of his theoretical discourse on non-violence, articulated in *Hind Swaraj*, and his narration on the 'invention' of non-violence in *Satyagraha in South Africa*.

In *Hind Swaraj*, the question of violence is dealt with only at the end of Chapter XIV, when the 'editor' Gandhi asks his interlocutor, the 'reader'—who upholds the point of view of the revolutionaries—how he intends to throw the British out of India by force. The question comes up because the revolutionaries preach armed struggle to put an end to British rule; Gandhi's position is purely reactive. The discussion focuses on the precedent of Italy, and in particular on the contrasting figures of Mazzini and Garibaldi, for whom the early Indian nationalists had a cult-like admiration. Gandhi, who had studied the question in great detail, refutes his opponent's argument and reminds him that, according to Mazzini, the War of Independence had not resulted in a real liberation of the Italian people but only in new forms of oppression. He then tackles the problem of arms, and puts forward two distinct arguments: first that arming the Indian people will take years; second that it would mean the europeanization of India and will therefore not be accepted by the Indian nation. His opponent replies that it is not necessary to arm the masses, that the struggle can start with a small group and a few assassinations, and that the next stage would be a generalized guerrilla warfare. Gandhi replies by stressing the immorality of these assassinations, singling out the murder of Sir Curzon Wyllie by Madanlal Dhingra. His opponent then emphasizes that such violence has forced the British to concede the Morley–Minto political reforms, and that this outcome clearly validates the use of violence. He goes on to develop an argument based on the necessary distinction between means and ends; for him, the end justifies the means.

This position is rejected by Gandhi via a long section where he argues that comprehension and pity are better arms than brute force. He takes the instance of a petition, the favourite weapon of moderate Congressmen, which draws sarcasm from his opponent. He himself acknowledges that, by itself, a petition does not get results, force is necessary. There are, however, two kinds of forces: brute force, which achieves nothing, and 'soul force' (satyagraha), which is irresistible. The use of brute force against the British could be justified only in the name of national interest. In this there is neither love nor pity, and it therefore cannot be invoked as a justification for action.

In the chapter that follows, his opponent asks Gandhi to give him instances of successful non-violent resistance. Gandhi's answer is that the existence of the world itself is testimony to the strength of the principle of love, because if violence had had the upper hand, the world would have been destroyed. But, Gandhi hastens to add, history, focusing only on violence, has kept no trace of this truth. The discussion then moves towards a general survey of non-violent resistance. Gandhi stresses that it implies self-sacrifice, which is infinitely superior to sacrificing others. To his opponent, who argues that this is a weapon of the weak, he retorts that it requires greater courage than violent struggle: 'A man without courage and virility cannot be a nonviolent resister.' He stresses that in India peasants have for a long time used forms of non-violent struggle. He then lists the qualities required of a resister, the first being chastity.

Interestingly, Gandhi's justification of non-violent resistance is not based on the notion of ahimsa. Religion is not invoked in this 1909 discussion, in which Gandhi first expressed his views on the question. In his presentation of his ethics of non-violence, Gandhi was careful to address three specific questions: that of unintended violence linked to everyday life, about which he acknowledged that there was no way of completely avoiding it; that of intentionality, on which he claimed that the limited use of violence could be justified by the need to prevent a greater harm; that of self-defence, which for Gandhi was, within certain limits, compatible with non-violence. His view of non-violence was not therefore predicated on metaphysical and religious consi-derations, but expressed in the language of pragmatic ethics.

The discussion on non-violence in *Hind Swaraj* apparently did not capture the attention of readers of the book, since, five years later, in an article in *Indian Opinion*, Gandhi himself deplored that the book had been seen in India as an incitement to anti-British violence! Such misunderstanding can be partly explained by the mode of exposition chosen by Gandhi, that is, the 'socratic' dialogue which, handled without Plato's agility, could misfire and give rise to confusion. A more probable explanation is that the sheer violence of Gandhi's own broadside against European civilization tended to limit the acceptability of his call to non-violence, which must have been perceived by many of his readers as a purely rhetorical device.

The exact circumstances in which Gandhi 'invented' satyagraha have been frequently narrated, first by Gandhi himself in *Satyagraha in South Africa*, a narration often plagiarized by later biographers but rarely analysed by them. If we refer to Gandhi's text, the 'invention' of satyagraha took place within a whole set of revelations which were to change the course of his life. During a one-month period of service as an ambulance worker in a small military campaign waged by the British against a Zulu uprising in 1906, Gandhi experienced a double revelation: that a man who aspires to a life of service must make vows of celibacy and must accept poverty for the whole of his life. When he came back to Johannesburg after the end of the campaign, he was informed of the promulgation of the 'Black Act' (Transvaal Asiatic Amendments Act), which appeared to him to pose a deadly threat to Indians in South Africa. He wrote:

> I clearly saw that this was a question of life and death for them. I further saw that even in the case of memorials and representations proving fruitless, the community must not sit with folded hands. Better die than submit to such a law. But how were we to die? What should we dare and do so that there would be nothing before us except a choice of victory or death? An impenetrable wall was before me, as it were, and I could not see my way through it . . .[7]

In his meeting with some of the leaders of the Transvaal Indians, he explained the measure in detail. They were as indignant as Gandhi himself. He told them that on their response hung the fate of Indians not only in the Transvaal but in the whole of South Africa:

[7] Gandhi, *Satyagraha in South Africa*, op. cit., p. 99.

If we fully understand all the implications of this legislation, we shall find that India's honour is in our keeping. For the Ordinance seeks to humiliate not only ourselves but also the motherland. The humiliation consists in the degradation of innocent men. No one will take it upon himself to say that we have done anything to deserve such legislation. We are innocent, and insult offered to a single innocent member of a nation is tantamount to insulting the nation as a whole. It will not, therefore, do to be hasty, impatient or angry. That cannot save us from this onslaught. But God will come to our help, if we calmly think out and carry out in time measures of resistance, presenting a united front and bearing the hardship, which such resistance brings in its train . . .[8]

The next stage was to hold a meeting in a Johannesburg theatre. A Muslim merchant, Seth Haji Habib, addressed the crowd and proposed that each participant swear by God that he would refuse to be subject to such a law. Gandhi acknowledges that he was, at first, surprised by Seth Haji Habib's suggestion, but that he then supported it enthusiastically. He drew the attention of the audience to the gravity of such a solemn commitment and did not hide from them the dangers they would face. But he declared he had confidence in the final victory, even if only a handful of men remained faithful to their oath to the end. The campaign started, and Gandhi forged the term 'satyagraha' as a substitute for 'passive resistance', which had been used by commentators.

An even cursory analysis of this narration shows that the context in which satyagraha was born had nothing to do with the one in which non-violence was discussed in *Hind Swaraj*. There did not exist, among South African Indians, a 'party of violence' advocating a different path, which in turn Gandhi opposed. For the Indians of South Africa, a small disarmed minority, violence was not an option. The importance of Gandhi's intervention lay in his ability to transform a discourse founded on a realization of weakness into an ethical one. Instead of presenting the form of struggle chosen as a weapon of the weak, and of trying to derive from it a moral advantage by playing on the existence of a degree of bad conscience among the Whites of South Africa, Gandhi chose to occupy the moral high ground by reaffirming the adequacy between the means and the ends of the struggle. Satyagraha was not born primarily from a refusal of violence, but

[8] Ibid., p. 101.

rather from a positive statement of moral strength. Only at a later stage, when confronted with terrorist circles upholding armed struggle against the British, did Gandhi oppose the moral strength of satyagraha to the brute force of terrorism.

It could be argued that Gandhi weakened his own position by putting on the same plane, as two opposed paths, violence and non-violence. From 1909 onwards, Gandhi's discourse on satyagraha had been of a dual nature, which resulted in a certain amount of confusion. On the one hand, he held a 'positive' discourse which hailed satyagraha as the translation of moral force into action. On the other hand, he had a 'negative' or 'reactive' discourse which presented satyagraha as an alternative to violence. When he wrote in the mid-1920s about his beginnings in South Africa, Gandhi was however able to rediscover the original inspiration of satyagraha, without being influenced too much by the discourse on non-violence that he had developed in numerous later texts.

The 'invention' of satyagraha originated from the logic of a situation—that of Indians in Transvaal in the aftermath of the Boer War. These men, who had supported the British in their war because they hoped to be able to enjoy certain basic rights, were confronted with evidence of a deterioration in their political condition under the British régime. This profoundly offended both their moral sense and their notion of the implicit contract between subjects and rulers. Struggle became for them the only way to restore their wounded dignity. It acted as a kind of catharsis in which the participants directed their violence against themselves. But the question of political violence was not at the heart of the original problematic of satyagraha. The problem was to find a form of struggle which, without provoking massive and violent repression, would be sufficient to prevent the authorities overlooking it, and which would at the same time unite participants and prevent attempts at division. At this early stage, the invention of satyagraha was more a lexical innovation than the discovery of a radically new form of struggle.

The relative success obtained by the satyagrahi in South Africa was partly due to surprise: the South African authorities were at first caught completely unawares by the capacity for action displayed by Indians, whom they thought of as simple coolies devoid of any spirit of resistance. It took them a few years to grasp what was happening and, in the meantime, in the face of pressure from the British and Indian governments, they thought it wise to make a few concessions. In South Africa, satyagraha benefited from a favourable window of opportunity, which perhaps gave Gandhi an exaggerated idea of its potential.

One should underline that, at this stage, there was no proper Gandhian theory of non-violence, but merely a word, satyagraha, which has rather mistakenly been equated with non-violence in general. At a later stage in his life Gandhi evolved a more philosophical kind of argument around the notion of ahimsa, borrowed from Jainism, which was very influential in Gujarat, even among Hindus, and which stressed the essential oneness of ahimsa with truth. Gandhi's idea of an isomorphism between the two notions had its source in Tolstoi—as acknowledged by Gandhi himself. Although ahimsa undoubtedly occupies a very central place in Gandhian thought, Gandhi often stressed that there were limits to its applicability and criticized those who tended to make it a fetish: 'I would prefer India to use arms to defend its honour rather than see it become cowardly or remain an impotent witness to its own dishonour.' He always argued that violence was preferable to cowardliness and deplored the 'emasculation' of India, which seemed to him, as to many nationalists, one of the most nefarious consequences of colonization. He always held the profession of arms to be an honourable occupation for those whose calling it was, in conformity with the theory of varna. In his view, satyagraha was designed for those who were not meant to bear arms, who would then be able to defend their honour without recourse to unsuited and immoral means. But he saw it as a form of struggle which required discipline and courage, at least as much as armed struggle. In his ability to combine various forms of individual and collective action, Gandhi was astonishingly creative and innovative. But his capacity to adapt his methods of struggle to changes in the situation seems to reflect pragmatism more than a continuous theoretical deepening. Actually, to him the theoretical aspect was always second to the pragmatic. His rationalizations were mostly meant for himself and it would be inappropriate to focus too much on his role as a theoretician of non-violent action—as Joan Bondurant does for instance.

Gandhi did not present himself as an apostle of non-violence. He did not preach the doctrine of ahimsa as such, even to the satyagrahi. It was a personal philosophy and he did not think that, to be good satyagrahis, people had to share all his philosophical views. He often said that even an atheist could be a good satyagrahi. The idea of an apostolate of non-violence, with its clear Christian connotations, is a contribution of his Western admirers. Men such as Holmes and Rolland were pacifists, and they sought a methodology of political action which would exclude armed violence without implying the passivity which in Europe too often characterized non-violent movements.

Transforming Gandhi into an apostle of non-violence and into the inventor of a method of political struggle endowed with universal value implies a double operation. This consists first in singling out, artificially, one element in his thought which made sense only in relation to a whole; and second in cutting off his struggles from the historical contexts of South Africa and India, in which they were nurtured.

Nationalism and Non-violence in India in Gandhi's Lifetime: Myth and Reality

Gandhi's influence certainly helped in limiting the role of violence in India's independence struggle, but it did not altogether prevent violent episodes from occurring. The Moplah rising of 1921, at the time of non-cooperation, was marked by widespread violence against Hindu landlords and forced conversions to Islam, while 1930 saw a rising in Peshawar, the Sholapur riots, the Chittagong armoury raid, and Bhagat Singh's attack on the assembly. In 1942 the Quit India movement gave rise to widespread violence in north India for several months. Communal riots took place on a regular basis from 1926 onwards. In all these episodes, thousands of lives were lost, not to mention the widespread massacres of 1946–8 at the time of Partition, when hundreds of thousands perished. To claim that the period of Gandhian leadership of the nationalist movement was a period without violence is to succumb to a myth and ignore historical reality. Gandhi himself, it should be noted, was not all the time busy preaching ahimsa and condemning violence. He condemned some violent episodes, like Chauri-Chaura in 1922, but kept silent about others. He joined in the protests against Bhagat Singh's execution although he did not support his actions; nor did he formally condemn them.

The notion of a non-violent revolution in India under Gandhi's leadership has meaning only in a comparative framework. In comparison with most other national liberation struggles, and taking into account the huge population of India, the cost in human lives was relatively small.

The limited amount of violence cannot be attributed primarily to the influence of Gandhi's ideas either. The notion of Gandhi's primacy on this score has become received wisdom because of a tendency to decontextualize the events in India, and to accept a version in which Gandhi, as a knight in shining armour, defied and defeated almost single-handed the mightiest empire on earth, whose representatives were considerate enough to accept their defeat gracefully. This romantic picture of the triumph of Gandhian non-violence prevails because, instead of looking at the role of the real actors in the drama, one tends to view Gandhi's action in terms of the eternal struggle of good versus evil. What is overlooked is the convergence of various, even opposing, interests, that could find their advantage in a form of non-violent struggle. This does not imply that Gandhi himself was manipulated; he knew very well what he was after, and, on the whole, was able to deal with the various attempts at instrumentalizing him.

Those who had a vested interest in seeing the Indian independence struggle remain within the bounds of non-violence were, on the one hand, most Indian property holders, big and small, as well as most 'enlightened' sections of the British ruling circles. Partisans of violence were found among those who advocated terrorist methods, who remained a force in India till the early 1930s—a fact too often overlooked—as well as among diehard imperialists, who never became dominant after 1920 in the councils of government. As far as the masses were concerned, the question of non-violence did not seem very relevant to them. Those who accuse Gandhi, especially among the Marxist Left, of having prevented a violent popular revolution do not have very convincing arguments and their use of counterfactual analysis, on the basis of China and Vietnam, does not carry much conviction either. On the other hand those who praise Gandhi for having spared his countrymen the horror of a bloody revolution tend to neglect the high price Indian society has paid and continues to pay for the maintenance of the social status quo.

The victory in India by methods which excluded armed violence, while offering a clear contrast to the case of other colonial countries, owes as much to this convergence of powerful interests as to Gandhi's unique charisma. The relative absence of violence allowed a fairly gradual transition to independence which served to maintain the economic, social and political dominance of the entrenched who could have been threatened by a more chaotic process. It also limited internal fractures within Indian society—with the exception of the gap between Hindus and Muslims which, on the contrary, was made larger, with tragic consequences that are all too well known.

The victory gained by a non-violent nationalist movement is largely due to the specific balance of social and political forces as it existed in India in the 1920s and 1930s, in which a broad coalition was needed to trigger a clear evolution towards independence. Big industrialists as well as middle peasants, shopkeepers and landlords, all had something to gain from the Gandhian programme, which mixed radicalism and conservatism in a unique blend and satisfied the many without antagonizing the few. The success of non-violent methods of mass agitation was possible only because of the existence of this broad consensus, which allowed isolating the partisans of armed struggle as well as the collaborators of imperialism. Gandhi did not create such a consensus all on his own, but he helped in its emergence and kept it alive in the long term.

Given the fact that the British left India voluntarily in 1947, Gandhi is often credited with having, as it were, converted the British rulers to his point of view. One of satyagraha's main objectives is, after all, conversion of the opponent, who is not treated as an enemy. It can even be said to be the satyagrahi's main ambition not to annihilate, as in a war, but to convert through love. Is it then possible to argue that in India the British were destabilized by the Gandhian method of non-violent struggle and that the confrontation with Gandhi transformed them morally? There is no doubt that it created great difficulties for them, to the point that Viceroy Lord Irwin, who, as previously mentioned, was not inimical to Gandhi, could not help confessing, in a letter to the Secretary of State for India,[9] that the death of the Mahatma would be a great relief to him. But it is not obvious that non-violence, more than other factors, was particularly decisive in sapping the British will to stay. Gandhi's objective of disarming the adversary through love and eventual conversion was never really achieved. Perusal of the correspondence between the viceroys and the secretaries of state for India shows that Gandhi's action never really impinged upon the good conscience of the British rulers, nor dented their conviction of their own moral superiority. Even those viceroys who recognized the moral greatness of Gandhi's personality never seriously questioned the legitimacy of the British position. The decision by the British to quit India, taken only at the beginning of 1946, was due to a convergence of factors, mostly of a strategic and economic nature, among which Gandhi's action did not figure as prominently as romantic nationalist views would have us believe.

Thus, non-violent resistance would not by itself have resulted in the independence of India had it not been combined with other factors. This is not meant to diminish the historical role of Gandhi, but it must lead to a more balanced appraisal of the contribution of non-violence to India's independence. Outside India, Gandhi's impact was limited by the difficult relationship he had with the international pacifist movement.

Gandhi and the Pacifists

Gandhi's approach to the problems of war and violence was quite different from that of most pacifists. Although pacifists generally accepted that there was a direct link between internal violence and foreign wars, their reading of it could vary, and they focused almost exclusively on the struggle against war. In Gandhi's mind, the priorities were reversed; he was mostly preoccupied with 'internal' violence and thought that, once this had been eradicated, the 'external' violence of war would disappear. There remained, therefore, always some ambivalence in the relationship between Gandhi and American and European pacifists. Although these pacifists saw Gandhi as a potential ally, even a source of inspiration, they were critical of aspects of his policies. As

[9] Irwin to Wedgwood-Benn, 7 April 1930, British Library, Oriental and India Office Collections, Halifax Collection, Mss Eur. C 152/6.

for Gandhi himself, he always took care to keep a distance *vis-à-vis* the pacifists, though he showed sympathy for some of their ideas.

In spite of this there is a widespread tendency to see Gandhi as a pacifist. In fact, Gandhi's position in regard to armed conflict was, as we saw, not devoid of ambiguity. During the early part of his life he took part in armed conflicts, though in a non-combatant role, which showed that he accepted the idea that there were just wars. His raising of a unit of ambulance workers among the South African Indians to help the British during the Boer War was, however, when he still believed in the benevolent character of British imperialism. Later, when he had developed a fundamental critique of Western civilization and its militarism and largely lost his illusions about the Empire, he still supported the recruiting efforts of the British in India in 1918— which made him very unpopular. He made no bones about the fact that his support was largely of a tactical nature; in exhange for his support to the British war effort, he hoped to get political concessions, a hope which proved to be in vain. Even after he had broken with the British, his attitude towards armed conflict remained, often, at odds with that of the pacifists. His severe indictment of the Munich agreement as a capitulation galled them particularly. After the start of the Second World War he made every effort, in 1939–42, to avoid hampering the British war effort, although he had denounced the war in the name of non-violence. In 1942, when he was instrumental in having Congress vote the 'Quit India' resolution, he accepted, on Nehru's insistence, the insertion of a clause which made it possible for Allied troops to remain in India for the duration of the conflict. Generally, in spite of the hope some pacifists put in him, he did not significantly contribute in his lifetime to the struggle against war. In the 1930s, at the time of the rise of Fascism, the question of the exemplary nature of his struggle was openly posed.

The Exemplary Nature of Gandhian Non-violence

From the 1930s onwards, on the basis of the successes he had obtained in India, Gandhi put forward the view that his method of non-violent resistance was universally valid. The limits of this pretension to universality were however cruelly exposed when he faced the problem of

Fascism and Nazism. His position on these doctrines created a veil of mutual recrimination between him and some Western intellectuals who were, *a priori*, rather well disposed towards him. This comes out most clearly from his correspondence with German Jewish intellectuals regarding the fight against Hitler's persecution of the Jews. Probably not very well informed about the realities of the German situation under the Nazi régime, Gandhi thought he could advise German Jews to use non-violent resistance methods. Martin Buber's perplexity was conveyed in a letter to the Mahatma,[10] to which the latter had no very convincing answer. In 1940 Gandhi also wrote a letter to Hitler, asking him to abandon the path of violence: this appears rather quixotic today. A major problem was that Gandhi, as well as others, saw Fascism and Nazism as monstrous outgrowths of modern civilization rather than as *sui generis*. They seemed confrontable with 'normal' methods.

Fifty years after Gandhi's death, an assessment of non-violence as a method of struggle remains a hazardous enterprise. Few major political changes have occurred on the sole basis of non-violent methods. In South Africa, after the early 1960s, the African National Congress combined armed struggle with mass demonstrations to eventually achieve a self-dissolution of the apartheid régime. African-Americans also combined non-violent resistance with armed struggle (Malcolm X and the Black Pathers) to obtain civil rights denied them for a century after the abolition of slavery. Other examples of non-violent struggle often mentioned are the overthrow of the Marcos dictatorship by 'people's power' in the Philippines in 1986, and the fall of communist régimes in Eastern Europe. To credit all these movements with 'Gandhian' inspiration appears to be the outcome of a fairly superficial analysis. That some movements claimed a Gandhian inspiration to appear more legitimate should not hide the problems posed by such instrumentalization of Gandhi.

In a recent text Henri Stern, a French researcher well acquainted with India and Gandhi, proposes to distinguish 'legitimate' from

[10] M. Buber, 'Letter to Mahatma Gandhi', February 1939, in P. Meyer, *The Pacifist Conscience*, op. cit., pp. 269–82. See also B. Kling, 'Gandhi, Non-violence and the Holocaust', *Peace and Change*, 16 April 1991, pp. 176–96.

'illegitimate' uses of Gandhi.[11] His view is that both the American Civil Rights Movement and the South African anti-apartheid movement can legitimately claim to have been inspired by Gandhi, inasmuch as they both displayed an ethic of responsibility predicated on respect of the law—this being in conformity with Gandhi's teaching. On the other hand he sees the claim of anti-authoritarian movements, such as the anti-nuclear movement, to be influenced by Gandhi as not based on solid ground. For he holds that Gandhi was never anti-authoritarian, and always advocated a scrupulous respect for the law, even when he fought laws he deemed unfair. Stern's view seems to be basically that Gandhi's position, developed in a cultural context specific to India and even to Hinduism, is not easily transposable to a different context.

The merit of such an analysis is to draw attention to the difficulty involved in deriving from Gandhi some paradigm of universal value. It must be recognized that non-violent resistance can take different forms, depending on period and culture, and that the movement initiated by Gandhi is a case among others. There is no good reason to equate non-violence as a method with Gandhi and Gandhism, even if the Mahatma is the most illustrious practitioner of that form of struggle. If Gandhi survives as a political figure, and not only as a spiritual master, it is because he addressed certain fundamental questions about the relationship between ethics and politics that are not limited to the idea of non-violence.

[11] H. Stern, 'Gandhi ou le yoga de la citoyenneté', in *Préceptes de vie du Mahatma Gandhi*, Paris, 1998, pp. 7–22.

Conclusion

In a survey of some of the books published on the occasion of Gandhi's centenary, T.K. Mahadevan felt there ought to be a moratorium on writings about the Mahatma. It can safely be said that this has not happened: in the last thirty years, the literature on Gandhi has continued to grow exponentially (this book included), and no reversal of the trend is in sight. Heroes are always needed and Gandhi is one of those rare figures who can satisfy the need.

Although there has been some retreat from the hagiographical trend which dominated work on Gandhi and which found one of its last expressions in Attenborough's film, the dominant view of the Mahatma is still characterized by hero-worship. This is probably one of the reasons why historians, who are nowadays wary of heroes, have contributed only in a limited way to this abundant literature. With Gandhi, one is confronted with a figure whose historical role was considerable but who does not lend himself to the genre of the historical biography. He left behind an enormous number of writings but they are of little help in reconstructing his thought, which seems always reluctant to assume fixed form. Hence an overabundance of interpretations, from which it is difficult to make a rational choice. You can choose your own Gandhi by singling out from his writings the specific passages relevant to your needs—even if they can be contradicted somewhere else. As a result, anthologies have been compiled which give many different images of Gandhi.

The overall logic of his public career is not easy to decipher either: between his roles as a political leader and as a social reformer, the link is not evident. His very specific itinerary sets him apart from all his contemporaries in India; he did not belong to a well-defined generation of leaders. He was in fact the survivor of an earlier generation who found himself suddenly projected to the fore, in defiance of the laws of biology and political gravity. The long period of maturation he went through in South Africa makes the task of the biographer even more impossible because it adds spatial disjunction to temporal.

This is why it has seemed to me that a detour, via the analysis of images, can be of great heuristic value. This is first because of the extraordinary diversity of ways in which Gandhi was perceived in his lifetime, and of his extremely rich posthumous trajectory. This 'second life' of Gandhi is one which historians can come to grips with more easily than the first, sudden shifts being easier to detect here. A second reason is that it is precisely Gandhi's transformation into an icon that has caused his unusual longevity; his glory survived the fading of hopes generated by Indian independence, and more generally by the liberation of colonized people from imperial domination. In this lies an explanation of the difference between Gandhi's fate and that of other great figures of the twentieth century—Lenin and Mao organized their own transformation into icons (although Stalin helped with Lenin)—but their reputation did not survive the collapse of the ideology which underpinned it. Gandhi erected no monument to himself, except the masterwork of ambiguity which is the *Autobiography*. He was not carried on the shoulders of any definite ideology, not even nationalism. He can therefore be continuously reinvented according to the needs and fashions of the times, and this reinvention has been going on incessantly. He was revered for several decades as an apostle of peace and is now viewed as the great ancestral figure of ecology and alternative movements. The future certainly holds other Gandhis in store.

Starting with a study of the images of Gandhi, I have stressed the impoverishment in the representations of the Mahatma after his death, coinciding with his transformation into an icon. To create an icon implies classifying existing representations and rejecting some, so as to produce an image susceptible of worship. With Gandhi, Indian icon-makers worked on purifying his image of all accretions that suggested his Victorian kind of eccentricity. Gandhi, in this vision, had to be a true Indian hero. At the same time, in order to make him a martyr of secularism, such nationalists tended to obliterate his Hindu side. The official image of the Mahatma which is proposed to worshipful crowds is that of a holy man, the upholder of a religion which is at the same time universal and rooted in the Indian context, a perfect and infallible leader who, through the sheer magic of his example, inspired the masses and threw the British out of India.

A different image, the product of multiple and often contradictory interventions, holds sway in the West. This tends to tear Gandhi away from his Indian roots and make him a kind of global hero who draws a response in all cultures. This vision is partly predicated on a similarity between the trajectories of Gandhi and Christ. But the secularization of Western societies does not make them well disposed towards messianic figures, and the parallel is rarely used openly nowadays. It appears safer to see Gandhi as a forerunner of alternative movements and ecology, and to reinterpret his non-violence as a call to respect nature.

Beyond political instrumentalization, the iconic image of Gandhi is of a man of God steeped in austerity, sexually renunciate, meditating in his ashram, whom the assassin's bullet providentially transformed into a martyr. He appears a heroic and tragic figure to be worshipped from afar, because inaccessible in his sheer perfection. All the evidence available, however, points to the real Gandhi as being very different, a man tormented by sensuality till the end of his life, endowed with a formidable appetite for life and an enormous capacity for work, blessed with a great sense of humour (including towards himself), aware of his lapses but full of pride in himself.

The contrast between the icon and the flesh-and-blood individual is the result of selective memory. Outside India, in particular in the West, the historical figure of Gandhi as the father of Indian independence has been all but forgotten; his role as the initiator and organizer of the greatest of anti-colonial movements—which has been the focus of this book—has been pushed to the background by the extraordinary acceleration of history which has relegated decolonization to a kind of prehistory of humanity. On the other hand, in India the historical Gandhi continues to give rise to heated debates in intellectual circles. Two opposing conceptions of Gandhi's historical role are pitted against each other. For one school of intellectuals and scholars, Gandhi, despite all his eccentricities, was ultimately part and parcel of the project of a specific Indian modernity, and is rightly considered, in a non-iconic way, as the father of the nation—a sort of spiritual father. For another school, Gandhi has been hijacked by the upholders of nationalist modernity, but he was actually the representative of a specifically Indian, or even Hindu, communitarian vision opposed to modernity (modernity being a synonym of westernization). Gandhi's status is a function of the view held of what constitutes modernity in the Indian context; those who criticize modernity as a derivative process are sensitive mostly to Gandhi's role in critiquing it and tend to stress his opposition to the modernizing project of the nation-state. They perceive his historical role as characterized by a kind of tragic misunderstanding. In contrast, those who see a specific Indian form of modernity give Gandhi an important place in its genesis.

Beyond the often passionate debates about his historical role, which have found very little echo outside India, Gandhi's relevance in our globalized world is defined in relation to his invention and refinement of a method of political struggle which is generally, although incorrectly, known as non-violence. The Gandhian message is often lost in the midst of these various interventions. There is a tendency to confuse it with an irenic Christian message of love and universal brotherhood. What Gandhi demands, in fact, is that every individual should try to discover the source of violence in himself and refrain from blaming a system (capitalism) or a government. When the source of violence has been identified, a remedy will become possible. Gandhi's equation of war and industrial civilization has been reinterpreted, and it is impossible to speculate on what Gandhi would have made of the deployment of this equation, as an ecological manifesto, especially by those who continue to contest the reigning order of globalized capitalism.

Gandhi's susceptibility to being reborn or reinvented reveals the paradox that, fifty years after his death, even as India is led by a Hindu nationalist government dominated by the heirs of the man whose pen directly guided Gandhi's assassin, Gandhi appears more than ever to carry a message of hope for mankind. It is clear that the Gandhi we hear of has little to do with the flesh-and-blood man of whom Einstein said, in 1930, that the generations to come would hardly believe such a man had walked the earth.

Select Bibliography

This is not an exhaustive bibliography: as a rule, only those books and articles referred to in the text have been listed.

Bibliographical Works

Carter, A., *Mahatma Gandhi: A Selected Bibliography, Bibliographies of World Leaders, Number 2*, Westport, Connecticut, London, 1995.
Mc Carthy, R.M. and G. Sharp, *Non-Violent Action: A Research Guide*, New York, London, 1997.

General Books on India and its History

Dumont, L., *Homo Hierarchicus. The Caste System and its Implications*, Chicago, London, 1980.
Kulke, H. and D. Rothermund, *A History of India*, London, New York, 1998 (3rd edn).
Stein, B., *A History of India*, London, 1998.

Gandhi's Works

Gandhi, M.K., *The Collected Works of Mahatma Gandhi*, New Delhi, 90 vols, 1958–84.
———, *An Autobiograhy: The Story of My Experiments with Truth*, London, 1972 (1st edn, Ahmedabad, 1927).
———, *Hind Swaraj and Other Writings*, edited by A.J. Parel, Cambridge Texts in Modern Politics, Cambridge, 1997.
———, *Satyagraha in South Africa*, Ahmedabad, 1928.

Anthologies of Texts by Gandhi

Gandhi, M.K., *Village Swaraj*, Ahmedabad, 1962.

Correspondence

Gandhi et Romain Rolland, Cahier Romain Rolland, no. 19, Paris, 1969.

Books by Contemporaries

Agarwal, S.N., *The Gandhian Plan of Economic Development for India*, Bombay, 1944.

Ambedkar, B.R., *What Congress and Gandhi Have Done to the Untouchables*, Bombay, 1945.

Bose, N.K., *Studies in Gandhism*, Calcutta, 1940.

Doke, J.J., *M.K. Gandhi: An Indian Patriot in South Africa*, London, 1909 (new edn, New Delhi, 1967).

Dutt, R.P., *India Today*, Bombay, 1940.

Godse, N., *Why I Assassinated Mahatma Gandhi*, Delhi, 1993.

Lanza del Vasto, J.J., *Pèlerinage aux Sources*, Paris, 1943.

Nehru, J., *Jawaharlal Nehru's Speeches, vol. I, September 1946–May 1949*, New Delhi, 1949.

——, *The Discovery of India*, Delhi, 1994 (1st edn, 1946).

Rolland, R., *Mahatma Gandhi*, Paris, 1924.

Spratt, P., *Gandhism: An Analysis*, Madras, 1939.

Homage and Commemorations

Muzumdar, H.T., ed., *The Enduring Greatness of Gandhi. An American Estimate. Being the Sermons of Dr John Haynes Holmes and Dr Douglas S. Harrington*, Ahmedabad, 1982.

Radhakrishnan, S., ed., *Mahatma Gandhi: Essays and Reflections on His Life and Work*, London, 1939 (1st edn).

Biographies of Gandhi

Ashe, G., *Gandhi: A Study in Revolution*, London, 1968.

Brown, J.M., *Gandhi: Prisoner of Hope*, New Haven and London, 1989.

Drevet, C., *Gandhi, sa vie, son œuvre, avec un exposé de sa philosophie*, Paris, 1967.

Erikson, E.H., *Gandhi's Truth*, New York, 1969.

Fischer, L., *The Life of Mahatma Gandhi*, New York, 1950.

Green, M., *Gandhi: Voice of a New Age Revolution*, New York, 1993.

Nanda, B.R., *Mahatma Gandhi: A Biography*, Delhi, 1989 (1st edn, London, 1958).

Payne, R., *The Life and Death of Mahatma Gandhi*, New York, 1969.

Tendulkar, D.G., *Mahatma: The Life of Mohandas Karamchand Gandhi*, New Delhi, 8 vols, 1960–3 (2nd edn).

Other Books on Gandhi and Gandhian Thought

Bondurant, J.V., *Conquest of Violence: The Gandhian Philosophy of Conflict*, Princeton, 1958 (1st edn).

Brown, J.M., *Gandhi's Rise to Power: Indian Politics 1915–1922*, Cambridge, 1972.

Dalton, D., *Mahatma Gandhi: Nonviolent Power in Action*, New York, 1993.

Das Gupta, A.K., *Gandhi's Economic Thought*, London, 1996.

Edwardes, M., *The Myth of the Mahatma: Gandhi, the British and the Raj*, London, 1986.

Iyer, R.N., *The Moral and Political Thought of Mahatma Gandhi*, New York, 1973.

Jordens, J.T.F., *Gandhi's Religion: A Homespun Shawl*, Basingstoke, New York, 1998.

Juergensmeyer, M., *Fighting with Gandhi*, New York, 1984.

Mahadevan, T.K., *The Year of the Phoenix*, Delhi, 1982.

Namboodiripad, E.M.S., *Gandhi and the 'Ism'*, Delhi, 1959 (1st edn).

Parekh, B., *Gandhi's Political Philosophy: A Critical Examination*, Basingstoke, 1989.

Pyarelal, N., *Mahatma Gandhi: The Early Phase*, vol. I, Ahmedabad, 1965.

Swan, M., *Gandhi: The South African Experience*, Johannesburg, 1985.

Books on Specific Aspects

Bhattacharya, S., *The Mahatma and the Poet: Letters and Debates between Gandhi and Tagore 1915–1941*, New Delhi, 1997.

Carson, C., ed., *The Autobiography of Martin Luther King Jr*, London, 1999.

Chandra, B., *The Rise and Growth of Economic Nationalism in India. Economic Policies of National Leadership*, Delhi, 1966.

Clodd, B.E., *The Story of Creation: A Plain Account of Evolution*, London, 1888.

Cosslett, T., *The 'Scientific Movement' and Victorian Literature*, Brighton, 1982.

Fox, R.G., *Gandhian Utopia: Experiments with Culture*, Boston, 1989.

Haksar, V., *Civil Disobedience: Threats and Offers (Gandhi and Rawls)*, New York, Oxford, 1986.

Kaunda, K., *Zambia Shall be Free: An Autobiography*, London, Ibadan, Nairobi, 1962.

Latronche, M.F., *L'influence de Gandhi en France de 1919 à nos jours*, Paris, 1999.

Luthuli, A., *Let My People Go*, New York, London, 1962.

Mandela, N., *No Easy Walk to Freedom*, London, 1965 (1st edn).

Markovits, C., *Indian Business and Nationalist Politics 1931–1939*, Cambridge, 1985.

Meyer, P., ed., *The Pacifist Conscience*, Harmondsworth, 1966.

Naess, A., *Gandhi and the Nuclear Age*, Totowa, NJ, 1965.

Nandy, A., *At the Edge of Psychology. Essays in Politics and Culture*, Delhi, 1980.

———, *The Intimate Enemy. Loss and Recovery of Self under Colonialism*, Delhi, 1983.

Pouchepadass, J., *Champaran and Gandhi*, Delhi, 1998.

Rudolph, L.I. and S.H. Rudolph, *The Modernity of Tradition: Political Development in India*, Chicago, London, 1967.

Schumacher, E.F., *Small is Beautiful. A Study of Economics as if People Mattered*, London, 1973.

Sharp, G., *The Politics of Nonviolent Action*, Boston, 1973.

Tarlo, E., *Clothing Matters: Dress and Identity in India*, London, 1996.

Thoreau, *Political Writings*, ed. by Nancy L. Rosenblum, Cambridge, 1996.

Vidal, D., *Violence and Truth. A Rajasthani Kingdom Confronts Colonial Authority*, Delhi, 1997.

Articles

Amin, S., 'Gandhi as Mahatma. Gorakhpur District, Eastern UP 1921-2', in R. Guha (ed.), *Subaltern Studies III. Writings on South Asian History and Society*, Delhi, 1984, pp. 1–61.

Bess, M., 'Peace Through Social Transformation: Danilo Dolci's Long Range Experiments with Gandhian Nonviolence', in Bess, *Realism, Utopia and the Mushroom Cloud: Four Activist Intellectuals and their Strategies for Peace 1945–1989*, Chicago, London, 1993, pp. 155–217.

Chatterjee, P., 'Gandhi and the Critique of Civil Society', in R. Guha (ed.), *Subaltern Studies III. Writings on South Asian History and Society*, Delhi, 1984, pp. 153–95.

Gordon, L., 'Mahatma Gandhi's Dialogues with Americans', *Economic and Political Weekly*, vol. XXXVII, no. 4, 26 January–1 February 2002, pp. 337–52.

Guha, R., 'Gandhi and the Environmental Movement', in Guha, *An Anthropologist among the Marxists and Other Essays*, Delhi, 2001.

Juergensmeyer, M., 'Saint Gandhi', in J. Stratton Hanley (ed.), *Saints and Virtues*, Berkeley, 1987, pp. 187–203.

Kelly, P.K., 'Gandhi and the Green Party', in S. Mukherjee and S. Ramaswamy (eds), *Facets of Mahatma Gandhi*, vol. 1, New Delhi, 1994, pp. 341–54.

Kling, B.B., 'Gandhi, Nonviolence and the Holocaust', *Peace and Change*, 16, April 1991, pp. 176–96.

Kumar, R., 'Gandhi and India's Transition to Bourgeois Modernity', in *Addressing Gandhi*, New Delhi, 1995, pp. 25–32.

Orwell, G., 'Reflections on Gandhi', *Partisan Review*, 16 , January 1949, pp. 85–92.

Polak, H.S.L., 'Saint, Patriot and Statesman', in C. Shukla, *Gandhiji as We Know Him*, Bombay, 1945, pp. 33–46.

Stern, H., 'Gandhi ou le yoga de la citoyenneté', in *Préceptes de Vie du Mahatma Gandhi*, Paris, 1998, pp. 7–22.

Vidal, D., G. Tarabout and E. Meyer, 'Introduction. Pour une interprétation des notions de violence et non-violence dans l'hindouisme et dans la société indienne', in *Violences et non-violences*, études réunies par D. Vidal, G. Tarabout, E. Meyer, Paris, 1994, coll. *Purusartha*, pp. 9–21.

Index